Political Economy of Contemporary Italy

Drawing on Kaleckian and Kaldorian approaches, *Political Economy of Contemporary Italy: The Economic Crisis and State Intervention* explores the reasons behind the stagnation of the Italian economy from the 1970s and suggests policy solutions to ease the crisis.

The central thesis of the book is that from the early 1990s Italy experienced a constant reduction of both private and public investment which, combined with increasing labour precariousness and wage moderation, contributed to the decline of both labour productivity and economic growth. It is argued that lack of industrial policies amplified the problem of the poor macroeconomic performance, since Italian firms – small-sized and non-innovating – were incapable of staying competitive on the global scene. Net exports did not compensate for the decline of public spending, private investment and consumption. It is also shown that, in these respects, Italy presents an interesting case study with wider ramifications for it was involved in the global process of intensifying the neoliberal agenda but at a faster rate than other OECD countries. The book concludes with a call for an alternative economic policy in order to promote innovation, reduce unemployment and stimulate economic growth.

This book marks a significant contribution to the literature on the recent history of the European economy, Italian studies and the history of economic thought.

Nicolò Giangrande is economist and researcher at the Giuseppe Di Vittorio Foundation (Italy).

Routledge Frontiers of Political Economy

Explaining Wealth Inequality
Property, Possession and Policy Reform
Benedict Atkinson

The International Political Economy of the Renminbi
Currency Internationalization and Reactive Currency Statecraft
Hyoung-kyu Chey

Financialization of the Economy, Business, and Household Inequality in the United States
A Historical–Institutional Balance-Sheet Approach
Kurt Mettenheim with Olivier Butzbach

Economic Ideas, Policy and National Culture
A Comparison of Three Market Economies
Edited by Eelke de Jong

Political Economy of Contemporary Italy
The Economic Crisis and State Intervention
Nicolò Giangrande

Reconfiguring the China-Pakistan Economic Corridor
Geo-Economic Pipe Dreams Versus Geopolitical Realities
Jeremy Garlick

The Political Economy of Transnational Governance
China and Southeast Asia in the 21st Century
Hong Liu

For more information about this series, please visit: www.routledge.com/Routledge-Frontiers-of-Political-Economy/book-series/SE0345

Political Economy of Contemporary Italy
The Economic Crisis and State Intervention

Nicolò Giangrande

Routledge
Taylor & Francis Group

LONDON AND NEW YORK

First published 2022
by Routledge
2 Park Square, Milton Park, Abingdon, Oxon OX14 4RN

and by Routledge
605 Third Avenue, New York, NY 10158

Routledge is an imprint of the Taylor & Francis Group, an informa business

© 2022 Nicolò Giangrande

British Library Cataloguing-in-Publication Data
A catalogue record for this book is available from the British Library

Library of Congress Cataloging-in-Publication Data
Names: Giangrande, Nicolò, author.
Title: Political economy of contemporary Italy : the economic crisis and state intervention / Nicolò Giangrande.
Description: Abingdon, Oxon ; New York, NY : Routledge, 2022. | Series: Routledge frontiers of political economy | Includes bibliographical references and index.
Identifiers: LCCN 2021025755 | ISBN 9780367544423 (hbk) | ISBN 9780367544430 (pbk) | ISBN 9781003089322 (ebk)
Subjects: LCSH: Economics—Italy. | Italy—Economic policy. | Italy—Social conditions. | Italy—Economic conditions.
Classification: LCC HB109.A2 G497 2022 | DDC 330.0945—dc23
LC record available at https://lccn.loc.gov/2021025755

ISBN: 978-0-367-54442-3 (hbk)
ISBN: 978-0-367-54443-0 (pbk)
ISBN: 978-1-003-08932-2 (ebk)

DOI: 10.4324/9781003089322

Typeset in Times New Roman
by Apex CoVantage, LLC

To my wife and parents
with love

Contents

3 The effects of the university reforms on the labour market   55

Figures

Preface

This book deals with the Italian economic stagnation in a long-term historical pattern, covering the period from 1970 to 2013. The author approaches
this question on the grounds of the transformations of the labour market and
the industrial relations, as well as on the reforms of the educational system.

The main conclusion he drives is that the Italian crisis depends on wage
moderation. More than in other countries, Italy experienced a significant
reduction of the labour share in the period under consideration, which
negatively impacted the domestic demand and the rate of growth of labour
productivity.

This is an interesting research, which would be of interest to economists,
historians, politicians and unionists.

Lecce, April 2021
Guglielmo Forges Davanzati

About the author

Nicolò Giangrande holds a PhD degree in Political Economy at the Human and Social Sciences PhD Programme of the University of Salento (Italy), with a semester as visiting scholar at the University of Cambridge (United Kingdom). He has a master's degree in Economic Development at the University of Campinas (Brazil), a master's degree in International Relations at the University of Bologna (Italy) at the Buenos Aires campus (Argentina) and a bachelor and a master's degree in Political Science at the University of Salento (Italy).

Currently, he is economist and researcher at the Giuseppe Di Vittorio Foundation (Italy), professor and director of the *Cátedra Barão do Rio Branco* at the U:VERSE University Centre (Brazil) and teaching assistant in Political Economy at the University of Salento (Italy).

He is the author of several articles in books and journals, and he has participated as speaker at numerous national and international conferences.

Acknowledgements

First of all, I would like to thank Guglielmo Forges Davanzati for his contribution to my research on the Italian economic decline in a heterodox framework. I am also thankful to John McCombie for his support during my period as visiting scholar at the Department of Land Economy at the University of Cambridge (UK). I would also like to thank all the academics, economists and unionists for their useful suggestions, in particular: Philip Arestis, Andrea Califano, Michele Carducci, Mimmo Carrieri, Giorgio Colacchio, Waldir José de Quadros, Maurizio Franzini, James K. Galbraith, Vitantonio Gioia, Alessandro Isoni, José Dari Krein, Roberto Lampa, Terri Mannarini, Mario Pianta, Angelo Salento, Riccardo Sanna, Mario Tiberi, Giuseppe Travaglini, Pasquale Tridico, Leonello Tronti and Vincenzo Visco. The usual disclaimers apply.

Abbreviations

ADI	Association of PhD students and young researchers in Italy
AMECO	Annual macro-economic database of the European Commission
ANVUR	National Agency for the Evaluation of Scientific Research
BOT	Italy's ordinary Treasury bills
CCC	circular cumulative causation
CCNL	National Collective Bargaining Agreement
CGIL	Italian General Confederation of Labour
CISL	Italian Confederation of Workers' Unions
CONFINDUSTRIA	General Confederation of Italian Industry
CRUI	Conference of Italian University Rectors
CUN	National University Council
DC	Christian Democracy
EEC	European Economic Community
EMS	European Monetary System
EMU	Economic and Monetary Union
EPL	Employment Protection Legislation
EPR	Employment Protection regular workers
EPT	Employment Protection temporary contracts
EU	European Union
EUROSTAT	Statistical office of the European Union
FDV	Giuseppe Di Vittorio Foundation
FIOM-CGIL	CGIL's metal workers' union federation
FLC-CGIL	CGIL's knowledge workers' union federation
FP-CGIL	CGIL's public workers' union federation
ICTWSS	Institutional Characteristics of Trade Unions, Wage Setting, State Intervention and Social Pacts
IMF	International Monetary Fund

ISCED	International Standard Classification of Education
ISTAT	Italian National Institute of Statistics
LN	Northern League
MEF	Ministry of Economy and Finance
MISE	Ministry of Economic Development
MIUR	Ministry of Education, University and Research
MLPS	Ministry of Labour and Social Policies
MP	Member of Parliament
OECD	Organisation for Economic Co-operation and Development
PCI	Italian Communist Party
PDS	Democratic Party of the Left
PM	Prime Minister
PRC	Communist Refoundation Party
PSI	Italian Socialist Party
RSU	unitary workplace union structure
UDU	University Students' Union
UIL	Italian Union of Labour

Introduction

Starting from the studies of the sociologist Luciano Gallino, a long and intense debate on the Italian economic decline has developed in recent years. His work exposed the disappearance of Italy's industrial sectors (Gallino, 2003) and paved the way to a fervent academic and public dispute. This heated discussion, in which many scholars took part, finished abruptly with the Great Recession in 2008, and it has re-emerged only recently.

This broad debate on the decline did not achieve any consensus, either on the variables that indicated it (Milone, 2005) or on its causes (Petrini, 2003). There has been tension between those scholars attributing the Italian stagnation mainly to some single cause and those emphasising multiple causes.

Many scholars, indeed, tended to ascribe the Italian economic decline to:

1 *The adoption of the euro.* There are those scholars who deem that the entry of Italy in the single currency does not allow any devaluation of national currency, thus limiting the chance for growth via the increase of exports (Bagnai, 2016a) and others who consider that the decision is based on class interests aimed at changing the power relations between capital and labour (Moro, 2018b).
2 *The institutional weakness of Italy.* This interpretation is based on the argument that the duration of Italian Governments is too short compared to the executives of other EU countries and this, in turn, reduces the credibility of Italy with international markets and does not allow the completion of the structural reforms (Macchiati, 2016) such as labour market deregulation, the reforms of the welfare system and the liberalisation of goods and service markets.
3 *The high public debt.* This argument is based on the idea that debt growth is due to waste in the public sector (Alesina et al., 2019), such as wages for civil servants and excess spending on welfare. Its increase reduces the growth rate due to the so-called "crowding out effect"– that

DOI: 10.4324/9781003089322-1

is public spending that reduces private spending – and the "Barro effect", which means the reduction of private spending to cope with future tax increases.

4   *The rigidity of the labour market.* This thesis considers the protection of labour excessive and argues that greater labour market flexibility can overcome generational and geographical differences, thus leading to an increase in economic growth and a boost for employment (Ichino et al., 2004).

Unlike these dominant interpretations, I deem that the Italian economic decline is not determined by a single cause, but by multiple factors – the production structure (Berta, 2004; Garruccio, 2005; Landini, 2017), industrial relations (Baccaro and Pulignano, 2011; De Luca, 2013), demographic trends (Livi Bacci, 2017; Soro, 2006), labour policies (Altieri and Ferrucci, 2009), education policies (Raitano and Supino, 2005; Saracco, 2005) – that affected all the components of aggregate demand, and that the main indicator of the decline is the reduction, or stagnation, of the growth rate of labour productivity (Ciocca, 2003; Forges Davanzati and Giangrande, 2019c).

In this book, I will show that the Italian economic decline has a long-term trajectory (Bellofiore, 2001; De Cecco, 2012; Gomellini and Pianta, 2007) that begins at the end of the 1960s and has its greatest manifestation in the 1990s, with the implementation of wage moderation and fiscal consolidation policies that had a negative impact on the macroeconomic level, on the labour market and on the production structure.

Many of the problems of the Italian economy have deep roots, which are found in the late industrialisation of Italy (Bianchi, 2013). Some of them have become structural over time, like (i) high unemployment;[1] (ii) large-scale emigration[2]; (iii) deep North–South economic divide[3]; (iv) aversion to competition.[4]

Everything changed radically in the 1980s, when people began to think that even those sectors of the economy managed by the State could be delivered to the market. This deep transformation was based on a neoliberal agenda, which was implemented in different ways depending on the country.

I am talking about an ideology that has been introduced progressively and almost imperceptibly in Italy and, moreover, with a broad consensus (Barbagallo, 2009). There has been no explicit political programme, unlike the clear intentions of the British Prime Minister, Margaret Thatcher, and the President of the United States of America, Ronald Reagan (Felice, 2015).

The shift has been epochal. It is worth mentioning that the economic paradigm moved from conceiving capital as a generator of income and work to concentrating only on its reproduction (Salento, 2016). Both the nature and the duration of the process have therefore changed, moving from productive investments to pure financial speculation (Forges Davanzati et al., 2019) from the medium and long term to the very short term. In the Italian case, the so-called "technocrats' government" played a decisive role. Indeed, this is an Italian peculiarity sustained and made possible because it was supported by a process of *de-politicisation* of economic policy.

In fact, I will assume that the Italian economic policy is driven by "economic alarmism" (Caffè, 1972), that is by a widespread conviction – which is generated in academic circles and propagated by the media – that in certain historical circumstances a major economic problem must be solved. Accordingly, I will organise the exposition on three dimensions: (i) the alarmism on inflation (1970s–1990s); (ii) the alarmism on labour market rigidity (1990s–2000s) and (iii) the alarmism on the education mismatch (2000s–2010s). I consider that, even if these three alarmisms showed real problems, they were a necessary premise in order to implement economic policies which went in the direction of reforming the labour market and the education system and, more generally, to redistribute income and power to the benefit of the ruling classes. This strategy aimed to distort the economic situation, to inflate its negative aspects and to fabricate the impression of a continuous emergency about the economic condition, with excessive emphasis on a real problem which is presented as *the* most important problem to solve, in which everything should be sacrificed in favour of public debt reduction, cuts in public spending and wage moderation.

In this respect, the economic problem, which is at the basis of the alarmism, is independent of the distribution of income and power between social groups. Due to lack of any social and political conflicts, the economic policy proposed by the dominant group became the official economic policy implemented by the government, in the perspective of the mantra "there is no alternative". In fact, the definition of economic policy has been gradually taken away from the dialogue between parliament, political parties and social actors – such as trade unions and business organisations – and entrusted directly to technocrats coming from specific academic circles or linked to particular national, European and international economic institutions.

This book follows this latter line of thought, with a particular focus on two aspects. First, I will specifically deal with the effects of wage dynamics on the path of labour productivity and the rate of growth. In this respect, I will insert in the basic Post-Keynesian view the idea – derived from Kalecki – that economic policy is of a class nature, and I assume a Kaldorian theoretical perspective, where dynamic interaction between aggregate demand and the path of labour productivity is at the basis of economic growth.

These causes on the labour side interacted reciprocally as a mechanism of circular cumulative causation (CCC) (Kaldor, 1966; Myrdal, 1957) and, with the fiscal consolidation policies, made the aggregate demand collapse. In fact, the decline of the wage share and the increased precariousness[5] in the labour market have affected labour productivity and have greatly changed the employment composition and its quality. Additionally, they have raised the unemployment and inactivity rate, increased inequality and poverty and, finally, have reduced the workers' and unions' power.

I explore the consequences of the wage moderation policy within a Kaleckian and Kaldorian framework. In this context, I facilitate the cross-fertilisation between the class nature of economic policy and the relationship between the rate of growth of labour productivity and the output growth rate.

I draw from Kalecki (1943) and contemporary fiscal sociology (Streeck, 2005) the insight that the bargaining power of workers, organised in trade unions, and capitalists in the labour market reflects their bargaining power in the political field. Moreover, I will examine within the Kaleckian theory the issue of the double role of wages in the capitalist economy, that is, a cost for the individual firm but a component of aggregate demand via consumption (Bhaduri and Marglin, 1990; Hein, 2017; Kalecki, 1968, 1971).

Furthermore, I get from the Kaldorian theory the link between the rate of growth of labour productivity and the output growth rate, and the idea that the path of innovation is dependent on the dynamics of aggregate demand, according to the so-called *Verdoorn Law* (Verdoorn, 1949) or *Kaldor's second law* (Forges Davanzati, 2018; Kaldor, 1966, 1989; McCombie and Spreafico, 2016; Targetti, 1988).

This book is organised in three chapters:

1   In the first chapter, I will deal with the "alarmism" on inflation in Italy in the 1970s and the economic policy designed to fight it. I will show that after the wave of class struggle in that decade and the defeat of the unions starting from the second half of 1990s, union density began to decline and so did the wage share. Italian capitalists managed to modify income distribution to their own benefit, mainly by means of a divide-and-rule strategy (i.e. decentralising production in small units);

2   The second chapter tackles the effects of the labour market reforms on the employment rate and the path of labour productivity. I will emphasise the gap between the expected outcomes of these reforms (i.e. to increase the employment rate) and their actual outcome. In particular, based on official evidence, I will show that, in the period under consideration (1990–2013), the employment quality in Italy tended to decline, as a result of the wage moderation policy. I deem that (i) elimination

of wage indexation, (ii) the promotion of a decentralised bargaining system and (iii) labour market flexibilisation acted as the main components of an overall wage moderation policy that contributed to the deterioration of the macroeconomic framework;

3 The third chapter deals with the reforms of the university system in Italy. Also, in this case, I will focus on the gap between the expected outcome (i.e. to increase the graduates) and the actual outcome. In contrast to the dominant economic thought, this book concludes with the economic proposal of the State as the innovator of the first resort, which brings work and public policies back to the centre of the economic agenda. Indeed, the idea is based on the increase of public spending for research and development (R&D), which can increase domestic demand in a short-run perspective with positive outcomes in the long-run path of labour productivity.

As regards to the methodology used, the following remarks are in order:

1 All arguments are based on official data, mainly from the Italian National Institute of Statistics (ISTAT) and the Organisation for Economic Co-operation and Development (OECD). The reconstruction provided is also based on a re-reading of the recent Italian political history with reference to documents in archives – such as those of the Italian General Confederation of Labour (CGIL) and the General Confederation of Italian Industry (CONFINDUSTRIA).

2 The criticism of the mainstream view is an internal critique, that is criticisms based on the proposal of macroeconomic models with a different set of assumptions from those of the mainstream view. This methodological option is in line with Graziani's argument (1997) about those who, wanting to fight for another economic vision, strive to discover an error in the logical construction of the opposing school. Indeed, according to Graziani, the acceptance that the errors could be eliminated means that the theoretical construction we are criticising would be acceptable. On the contrary, following Graziani's insight, since there are opposing views, even if they have a meticulous formulation, each one must be incompatible with the other (Graziani, 1997).

3 The arguments presented earlier do not discuss the complex topic of the "variety of capitalism". I do not aim to sustain the view, nor to deny it, that Italian capitalism has special features which distinguish it from other institutional architectures (Gambarotto and Solari, 2014; Rangone and Solari, 2012). At the same time, I will use the category of neoliberalism in its broader sense, meaning a set of economic policies

which aims at deregulating both the labour market and the market for goods and services, while involving a massive State intervention for promoting increasing income inequality, mainly via fiscal and monetary policy (to the benefit of big firms and rentiers) and favourable taxation on high-income households and firms.

4   The choice of the period under investigation was influenced by the following considerations. In May 1970, following the demands of the "Hot Autumn" of 1969, the Statute of the Workers' Rights (Law no. 300/1970) was approved, giving rise to a period of intense class struggle and rise of the labour share. The period analysed ends in 2013, that is, the year in which CGIL published its economic policy proposal, conceived as a set of interventions designed to stop the Italian economic decline.

5   I will deal with the gap between the desired outcomes of wage moderation policies (i.e. to increase employment) and their actual results, as well as the gap between the expected and real effects of the education reform on the path of labour productivity. In particular, I will show that while these reforms were conceived for the purpose of increasing "employability" and raising the percentage of graduates, they achieved the opposite outcome.

Notes

1   On unemployment in Italy: for an overview, see Zucchetti (2005); for its history, see Alberti (2016); for long-term unemployment, see Reyneri (1995); for its evolution, see Pugliese and Rebeggiani (2004) and how to fight it see Gallino (1998).

2   For the history of internal migration from *Mezzogiorno*, which is composed of the south of Italy and the two main islands (Sicily and Sardinia), to Central and Northern Italy, see Ginsborg (2006). For the historical Italian migration abroad, see Franzina (2003); for recent migration, see Fondazione Migrantes (2019).

3   For the history of structural gaps of the *Mezzogiorno* with the rest of the country, and the public interventions to reduce them, see Bevilacqua (2005).

4   For the historical roots of Italy's competitive deficit and its consequences, see Gigliobianco and Toniolo (2017).

5   For a portrait of precarious workers, see Standing (2011); for an analysis of the precariousness in the Italian labour market, see Gallino (2014).

1 Social conflict, union density and the struggle against inflation

1.1 Introduction

This chapter provides an interpretation of the reorganisation of Italian capitalism from the 1970s to the beginning of the 1990s, based on the view that the long trade union defeat phase, which started at the beginning of the 1980s, has paved the way to the ensuing policies of wage moderation.

In so doing, I propose a reconstruction of recent Italian economic history based on the changes in industrial relations. Following Michał Kalecki, I will assume that trade unions' influence in the political arena depends on their bargaining power in the labour market. In other words, as the unions' bargaining strength in the labour market falls (e.g. as a result of increasing unemployment or precarious jobs) so does their capacity to affect the direction of economic policy. I will add that union action is profoundly affected by workers' collective memory and, therefore, by their learning. Indeed, past experiences of successful social conflicts are likely to push workers to join unions, expecting their action to lead to success.

This theoretical framework is used in order to analyse the changes in the political power of workers from the end of the 1960s to nowadays with reference to the Italian case. It will be shown that two main stages occurred:

1 In the years after the Second World War there are elements of weakness in the production structure and in Italy's specialisation, the latter being conditioned by foreign demand. In the international market competition, price factors have prevailed instead of technological ones (Gomellini and Pianta, 2007). The first period (1969–1980) of my analysis was characterised by increasing social conflict and increasing union density. This part started with the so-called *Hot Autumn*[1] and ended in Turin with the *march of 40,000*[2] FIAT employees, mainly from management and white-collar sectors. In this period, the trade unions became a political actor, able to influence economic policy and push income

DOI: 10.4324/9781003089322-2

distribution towards equality. For the sake of increasing their profit margins, Italian capitalism reacted to the social struggles of 1968–1969 using a "divide and rule" strategy, mainly through the decentralisation of production from the *Industrial Triangle*[3] to the *Third Italy*.[4] This process would encourage industrial fragmentation and strengthen the aspect of the Italian production system featuring micro- and small firms specialised in traditional sectors.

2 Facing difficulties in finding new internal equilibria after the social conflict, Italian economic development has relied on exports as the engine of growth. Indeed, the second phase (1980–2013) of my analysis was marked by a strong capitalist counteroffensive, which decreased the degree of solidarity among workers and therefore caused a decline in union density. The drop of the trade unions' political power opened the way to wage moderation, implemented in order to support exports. The view that inflation had been generated by the trade union actions was the basic motivation for this strategy, and the struggle against inflation became the fundamental aim of the government of this period. A long period of continuous wage decline began and, as will be shown, this was one of the most important factors triggering the so-called "Italian economic decline" in the ensuing decades.

In the period under consideration, the rate of growth of real wages was faster than labour productivity. If labour productivity grows less than real wages this involves a decline of the rate of profits.[5] Evidence shows that this occurred in Italy in the 1970s. Italian firms reacted by trying to increase their bargaining power, according to the ways described in the next section, and also tended to increase their speculative activities in order to respond to the decline of industrial profits, as shown by Salento and Masino (2013) and Forges Davanzati et al. (2019).

The link existing between the dynamics of wages and that of labour productivity is ambiguous and depends on the historical and institutional setting. In the period under consideration, the rise of wages was driven by social conflict, while that of labour productivity was driven by both public and private investments.

Based on the available evidence, some stylised facts of the Italian economy can be considered:

1 The increase in the inflation rate was not to be entirely blamed on the money wage rise: the increase in tariffs and in the price of raw materials, oil above all, significantly contributed to this dynamic (Graziani, 2000; Leon, 2017). A reasonable explanation of this fact is that Italian inflation in the 1970s was a case of *conflictual inflation*, involving both a conflict over income distribution between workers and capitalists and an intercapitalist conflict: the latter between countries specialised in

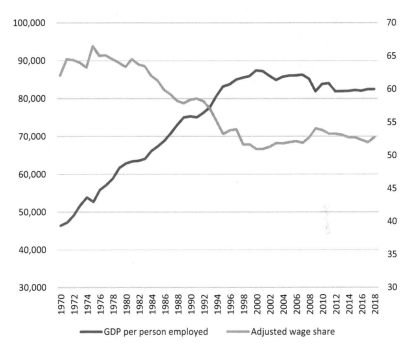

Figure 1.1 GDP per person employed (USD, constant prices, 2010 PPPs, left) and
adjusted wage share as percentage of GDP at current prices (compensa-
tion per employee as percentage of GDP at market prices per person
employed, right) (1970–2018)

Source: My elaboration on OECD and AMECO data

the production of manufactured goods and countries specialised in the
export of raw materials (i.e. a conflict between capitalists and rentiers).

2   The labour productivity trend, driven by both public and private
investments in a context where big firms – both private and public –
existed, was still much higher than that of ensuing decades in Italy (cf.
Chapter 2).[6] The main factor which slowed its dynamics can be traced
in the effects of the devaluation of the Italian lira. As emphasised by
Graziani, this acted as an incentive for firms to compete via cutting costs
in international trade and not via innovation (Graziani, 1997, 2000).
Moreover, the increase in labour productivity could be also imputed to
the increase in wages. This effect, labelled the *high wage theory*, was
elaborated, among others, by Francesco Saverio Nitti, an Italian economist of the second half of the nineteenth century. Nitti stressed that an

increase in wages stimulates the increase in the rate of growth of labour productivity (Forges Davanzati and Patalano, 2015), in view of the following factors: (i) a nutritional effect (i.e. higher wages allow workers better nutrition); (ii) a motivational effect (i.e. wage rises allow workers to work harder); (iii) a technological effect (i.e. wage increases stimulate firms to innovate). Although the high wage theory states that as wages rise labour productivity grows, in the period under investigation a different effect was in operation: wages grew faster than labour productivity.

3   Italian firms obtained their (decreasing) profit margins by increasing prices in the domestic market, while they made profits in foreign trade by means of the devaluation of the lira. Moreover, Italian firms tried to increase their profit margins using divide and rule strategies, as it will be shown in Section 1.2.[7]

The exposition is organised as follows. Section 1.2 shows the decline of union density in Italy and elaborates on evidence regarding the Italian case starting from 1969 until 2013. Section 1.3 analyses the alarmism on inflation. Section 1.4 studies the positions of the largest Italian trade union confederation, the Italian General Confederation of Labour (hereafter referred to as CGIL, according to its initials in Italian) on the tripartite agreements signed in July 1992 and July 1993. It relies on the *Rassegna Sindacale* (CGIL's weekly publication) and institutional memoranda. Section 1.5 deals with CGIL's economic proposals on development.

In the next sections, all references made to the "trade unions" will refer to the three main Italian trade union confederations: the CGIL, the Italian Confederation of Workers' Unions (CISL) and the Italian Union of Labour (UIL).

1.2 The decline of union density in Italy

The long Italian stagnation, as will be shown in the following sections, basically depends on wage moderation, which, in turn, depends on the continuous loss of bargaining power of the Italian trade unions, both in the labour market and in the political arena. This section aims to provide an interpretation of this phenomenon starting from the view that membership and participation in the trade unions depend on many factors such as political (Hyman, 2001), organisational (Cella, 2004) and cultural issues (Bernaciak et al., 2015). Normally, union membership is characterised by highs and lows, and it can differ among production sectors and geographical areas.[8]

In other words, I support the view that it is the existence of a working class with strong links of solidarity (and cultural and political support) which affects the decision to join the union. In such a situation, union density increases because workers "learn", and learning refers to the collective and dynamic "memory" of unions' successful experiences. As unions obtain the desired outcome (e.g. wage rises, reduction of inequalities), this is absorbed by the workers' memory and pushes them to join the union.

In this respect, I reverse the standard mainstream view: it is not the expected benefit deriving from union action which affects the individual decision to join a union, but *past experience* (Crouch, 2017). I argue that this approach can be appropriate to study the variation of union density in Italy in the period at stake, taking the evidence into consideration.

In this section, I will analyse in a diachronic way the development of:

1 labour disputes, the workers participating in the confrontations and the non-worked hours due to disputes through the data provided by ISTAT (1949–2009);
2 union density, that is, the percentage of workers who join unions on the total number of active workers through the data provided by the Institutional Characteristics of Trade Unions, Wage Setting, State Intervention and Social Pacts (ICTWSS) database (1960–2018) elaborated by Visser (2019).

The peaks in the number of labour disputes were reached at different times (Figure 1.2). In the agricultural sector, the peak was reached in 1954

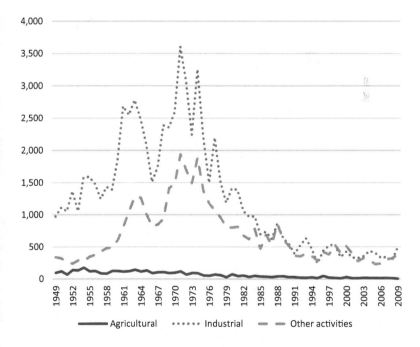

Figure 1.2 Labour disputes in Italy (1949–2009)

Source: My elaboration on ISTAT data

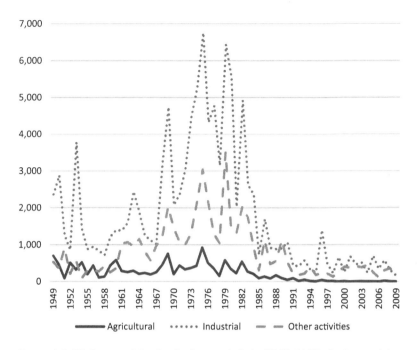

Figure 1.3 Workers participating in disputes in Italy (1949–2009) (in thousands)
Source: My elaboration on ISTAT data

with 174 disputes, while in the industrial sector and other activities it was reached in 1971, respectively, with 3,605 and 1,937 disputes. The lowest points were recorded in the industrial sector in 1995, with 244 confrontations, in other activities in 2005, with 231 disputes, and in the agricultural sector in 2009, with six disputes.

Until 1974, disputes unrelated to work are also included, while after 1975 these data were measured separately and excluded from the total. From 1986 onwards, "other activities" was broken down into two sets of data ("services" and "public sector"), of which it is the sum. Moreover, from 1998 onwards, the "public sector" also covered data on education and health systems.

Workers' participation in the disputes in Italy reached its peak in both the agricultural and industrial sectors in 1975, with 922,000 and 6.8 million workers, respectively, while their lowest points were in 2009, with 2,000 and 171,000 workers (Figure 1.3). In the "other activities" sector, the lowest point came in 1954, with 87,000 workers, and the highest point in 1979, with 3.5 million.

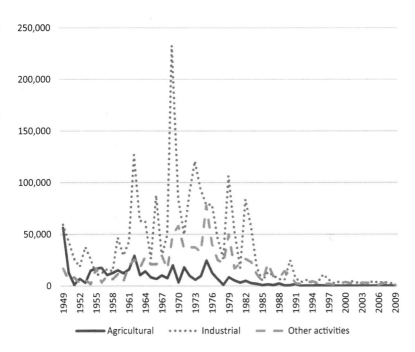

Figure 1.4 Non-worked hours due to disputes (1949–2009) (in thousands)
Source: My elaboration on ISTAT data

The non-worked hours due to disputes (Figure 1.4) were at the highest point in 1949 in agriculture (56.3 million), in 1969 in the industrial sector (almost 232.8 million) and in 1975 in the other activities (almost 78 million hours). The lowest points were reached for all three sectors in the twenty-first century, respectively, in 2001 (agriculture: 14,000), in 2009 (industry: 1.5 million) and in 2006 (other activities: 862,000).

In summary, in Italy's history, the highest points in these three aspects of labour relations conflict occurred from 1969 to 1975, while the lowest points were reached from 1995 to 2009. Indeed, the most non-worked hours due to a dispute occurred in 1969, which corresponded with the aforementioned *Hot Autumn* (302.6 million). The highest total of labour disputes (5,598) and the most workers participating in disputes (10.7 million) were, respectively, in 1971 and 1975. In 1995, labour disputes were at their lowest point (545), while the smallest number of workers participating in disputes (267,000) came in 2009, along with the fewest non-worked hours due to a dispute (2.6 million). However, the total amounts shown in Figures 1.5–1.7

Figure 1.5 Total labour disputes in Italy (1949–2009)

Source: My elaboration on ISTAT data

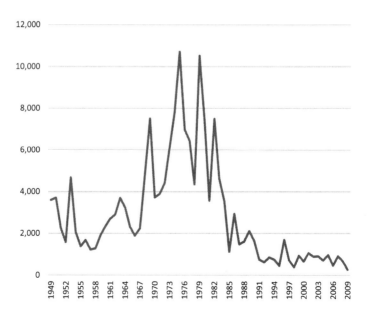

Figure 1.6 Total workers participating in disputes in Italy (1949–2009) (in thousands)

Source: My elaboration on ISTAT data

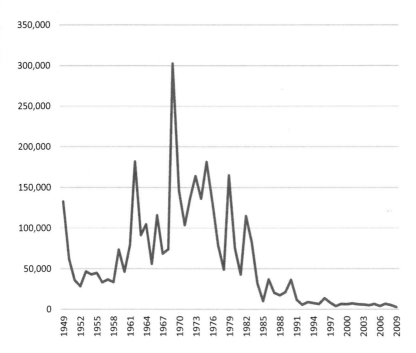

Figure 1.7 Total non-worked hours due to disputes (1949–2009) (in thousands)
Source: My elaboration on ISTAT data

could be less than the sum of the disputes per sector due to the different durations and the participation of workers from several sectors.

The data on union density in Italy is analysed in Figure 1.8 from data provided by the ICTWSS database.

As shown, the peak point of union density in Italy was in 1976, seven years after the 1969 *Hot Autumn*,[9] which was the period of the most intense conflict and also the richest in terms of achievements such as higher wages and better welfare (Pepe et al., 2003).

Evidence seems to support the view that the dynamics of union density is driven by collective learning and also depends on the variations of relative bargaining power of capital and labour both in the labour market and in the political arena (Kalecki, 1943). In particular, the Italian case, as described by the evidence mentioned earlier, suggests that a *path-dependent theory of union density* was in operation, and that it developed in the following steps:

1   A significant exogenous episode of social conflict generates a modification of income distribution to the benefit of workers.

Figure 1.8 Union density in Italy (1960–2018)
Source: My elaboration on ICTWSS database

2   Unions react by intensifying their claims. As this action is successful
    (i.e. a further income redistribution in workers' favour is implemented),
    the fact that union action is profitable starts to be recorded in the mem-
    ory of workers, who join the union collectively.
3   The subsequent increase in union density allows workers to obtain fur-
    ther benefits, in terms of wage rises and of increasing political power
    and, therefore, of the possibility of influencing economic policy.
4   The subsequent profit squeeze forces capitalists to react in order to
    reduce workers' bargaining power. The capitalists can use different
    strategies according to the specific historical and institutional setting
    of the country, and it may also involve economic policy interventions.
    Capitalists may use many devices such as labour market deregulation,
    increasing taxation on labour, decentralised wage bargaining, produc-
    tion transfers or the threat of *capital strike* (Salvati, 2000). Importantly,
    the "divide and rule" option is fundamental in order to reduce the
    degree of solidarity among workers and, consequently, to reduce the

unions' bargaining power (Braverman, 1998), allowing for a "sudden stop" to social conflict.

5 Once this strategy proves to be successful, the unions' bargaining power in the political field declines and so does the wage share. At the same time, income distribution changes to the detriment of workers. As a result, the room for bargaining is reduced for the union, involving its transformation from a *political actor* (Di Bartolomeo and Papa, 2017) to a *market agent* (Streeck, 1992). Workers begin to internalise *individualistic* habits of thought as a result of the reduction of the degree of solidarity among workers. In the end, social conflicts decline and so does union density.

The weakness of the degree of solidarity among workers involves the adoption of habits of thought which increase competition among workers in the labour market. This, in turn, allows capitalists to cut wages and to restore their desired normal rate of profits.

Accordingly, contrary to the mainstream narrative, which bases the unionisation process on individual analysis of expected benefits and current costs (Boeri and Checchi, 2001), I propose a reversal of causation. This means that it is the benefits already obtained that motivate union membership and that the decision is influenced by the effects of dynamic memory and collective learning. On the empirical level, it is shown that union density (Visser, 2019) increases as an outcome of successful union disputes, and this link can explain a kind of learning effect on social groups, workers in particular. So, the existence of a workers' *memory* suggests that unionisation decisions at time t are affected by successful union disputes at time t_{-1} and, on the contrary, that the decline in union density in most OECD countries, and in Italy in particular, also depends on cases of failure of trade union action.[10]

This theoretical framework is based on the view that economic agents learn from past events and that economic variables move in a continuous time span. It is maintained that in the event an exogenous variable (X_t) varies, its variation has a permanent effect on the path of an endogenous variable (Y_t). As regards the issue examined here, this means that when social conflict has a successful result, workers learn that trade unions' action is effective for reaching their aims (e.g. for the aim of increasing the labour share and improving income distribution), and thus they tend to join a union.

In the Italian case, the dramatic decline of both social conflict and trade union action started in the early 1980s. This reflects a radical change of power relationships between capital and labour and, as will be shown, allows Italian firms – and their main representative organisations – to demand an overall policy of wage moderation from the government. The theoretical basis for this request relied on the alarmism about inflation. The high inflation rate in Italy in the 1970s and 1980s was imputed to the excessive increase in money wages and, in order to counteract it, trade union bargaining power had to be significantly reduced. The next section deals with this topic.

1.3 The alarmism about inflation

The bargaining power of trade unions was thus weakened, and inflation – which in the previous years was extremely high also because of the double oil shock of 1973 and 1979 – began to shrink. After the peak reached in 1980 (21.2%), the inflation rate continued to decline during the 1980s, reaching 4.7% in 1987 (Figure 1.9). On one hand, this happened at the end of the period of conflict inside and outside firms and at the beginning of a phase of wage moderation. On the other hand, the interest rate increased because of the Treasury/Bank of Italy "divorce" and in order to attract speculative capital to rebalance the balance of payments.

Contrary to expectations, the interest rate increase had a negative effect on the dynamics of private investments, which were not offset by public

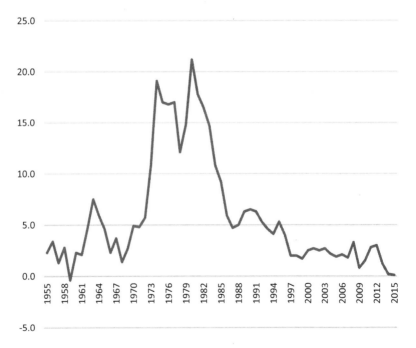

Figure 1.9 Percentage changes in the National Index of Consumer Prices in Italy (1955–2015)

Source: My elaboration on ISTAT data

investments. The 1980s were characterised by an increase in public debt not attributable to increases in social spending. In fact, the increase in public spending was predominantly due to an increase in current expenditures, ending with the definitive neutralisation of the social conflict inherited from the previous decade.

Italy's admission to the European Monetary System (EMS)[11] in 1979 introduced more constraints on the national monetary policy, preventing competitive devaluations, leading firms to be more rigid. This external constraint should have encouraged competition based on productivity growth, but Italian firms reacted by continuing to reduce costs and first of all wages.

There are two important government measures at this stage:

1   The so-called "divorce" between the Ministry of the Treasury and the Bank of Italy in 1981, when the Central Bank was no longer allowed to buy all the public debt bonds that were unsold on the market (Andreatta et al., 2011). This decision was designed to contain the dynamics of public debt, but, on the contrary, it led to its explosion (Figure 1.10) by raising interest rates. Meanwhile, economic growth due to increased

Figure 1.10 Percentage of public debt on GDP in Italy (1949–2015)

Source: My elaboration on IMF data

consumption was possible mainly through the high interest rates on savings. In other words, Italian households of the period benefited from the high interest rates on State bonds, which allowed them to increase the wealth deriving from their accumulated savings and hence to maintain a rising level of consumption. In the Italian political debate of that period, those households were buying Italy's ordinary Treasury bills (BOT) and were labelled "BOT-people",[12] meaning that their consumption was possible because they were creditors of the State (Forges Davanzati and Pacella, 2010).

2   The so-called "Saint Valentine's decree", issued on 12 February 1984, by the first government led by the socialist leader Bettino Craxi (1983–1986), designed to contain wage growth by modifying the automatic wage indexation mechanism (in Italian *scala mobile*) with the official motivation of reducing the inflationary pressure (Benvenuto and Maglie, 2016; Carniti, 2019; Trentin, 2017).

The combination of the two main measures mentioned earlier has generated an increase in inequality, starting a radical change – over the past decade – based on the effects of trickle-down economics.

In the 1990s there began a turbulent period that involved political, economic and financial crisis, determined by the changes in the domestic and international context.

This phase originated in the 1980s and was caused by three main factors (Graziani, 2000), which led to a weakening of Italian industry: (i) the Asian Tigers (Hong Kong, Singapore, South Korea and Taiwan) joined the global market; (ii) the gradual enlargement[13] of the European Economic Community (EEC) to Southern Europe (Greece, Spain and Portugal) – and its subsequent transformation into the European Union (EU); (iii) German reunification.

Indeed, the newly industrialised Asian countries and the new EEC countries became direct competitors of the Italian production system but with lower labour costs. Moreover, once the Berlin Wall was torn down in 1989 and the Cold War ended in 1991, Italy was no longer a strategic country in the international scenario. As a result, Italy quickly lost its status as recipient of loans from the United States and West Germany. The United States started to look more to the Eastern European countries in order to contain Russia, and West Germany managed to completely reacquire its political status and re-establish its full economic strength in the middle of the European continent after having rapidly re-absorbed East Germany (Castronovo, 2013).

On top of these three events that put pressure on the Italian production system in terms of labour costs, technological advancement capabilities and the attraction of capital funding, it is worth adding the Maastricht Treaty. It was signed on 7 February 1992, by Gianni De Michelis, Italy's Foreign Affairs Minister, and Guido Carli, Italy's Treasury Minister. This treaty transformed the EEC into the EU and laid the foundations for the creation of a single currency by 1999. Since the European countries had various differences in the fundamentals – such as inflation rate, productivity, balance of payments, public debt and expenditure – they needed to rebalance their own budgets to achieve the parameters set for participation in the single currency. In Italy, this meant abrupt economic measures composed of public spending cuts, a tax hike and the selling off of public assets.

The profound international changes with the appearance of new global players and the Maastricht Treaty requirements therefore exerted pressure not only on Italy's economy but also on its political system. This combination led to the end of the political consensus based on rising government expenditure financed by the growing public debt.

On the domestic side, the beginning of the *Mani Pulite* investigation,[14] the result of 1992 general election[15] and the bombing attacks by the Sicilian mafia[16] provoked the irreversible crisis of the traditional Italian party system. Moreover, the main government parties, such as Christian Democracy (DC) and the Italian Socialist Party (PSI), were weakened by the movement which, through the referendum, tried to change the electoral system into a majority system in order to renew the political class and to allow a real alternative (Galli, 2004; Lepre, 2006).

The year 1992 was also a presidential election year, being the end of Francesco Cossiga's term. Following the incumbent President Cossiga's resignation, the then-President of the Chamber of Deputies Oscar Luigi Scalfaro was elected on 28 May 1992. In the middle of the political and economic crisis, Scalfaro appointed Giuliano Amato as President of the Council of Ministers (hereafter referred to as "Prime Minister" or, abbreviated, "PM") on 28 June 1992. It was the first Italian Government with a significant presence of technocrats as the key ministers.

Faced with an overall emergency, PM Amato and his Treasury Minister, Piero Barucci, planned an urgent fiscal consolidation plan to the tune of 93 trillion Italian lira, which was implemented by cutting public expenditure (43.5 trillion), increasing taxation (42.5 trillion) and privatising the main State-owned companies (7 trillion) (Pesole, 2010). This was the first tough austerity measure, defined by the same PM as a "tears and blood" balancing plan, implemented with the aim of reducing public debt and avoiding future speculative attacks against the lira, which had already forced the government to devalue the currency and leave the EMS on 16 September 1992.

In order to tackle the rising inflation, the Italian Government decided to promote tripartite talks with the largest workers' and employers' organisations. This negotiation was supported first by the Minister of Labour of the seventh Andreotti government, Franco Marini – who was former CISL General Secretary (1985–1991). Later, when the government led by Amato was in office, it was pursued by the PM himself and his Minister of Labour, Nino Cristofori. The tripartite agreement – better known as *Amato Protocol* – was signed on 31 July 1992 by the main trade unions and employers' confederations, and it put an end to the automatic wage indexation mechanism. In summary, the wage moderation process that had started with the so-called "Saint Valentine's decree" was now complete.

The objective was to neutralise the wage dynamics originating in the price–wage spiral. Actually, inflation had already changed in the 1980s because it was no longer wage inflation, but imported inflation and inflation caused by interest rates, tariffs and taxes (Graziani, 2000).[17] As we can see in the next section, the manner in which this agreement was concluded led to a deep rift within the CGIL.

In 1993, always within an economic and political crisis, President Scalfaro appointed Carlo Azeglio Ciampi as PM on 28 April 1993. Ciampi had been serving as Bank of Italy Governor until that moment and became the first non-member-of-parliament (non-MP) to lead a cabinet in the history of the Italian Republic. Ciampi's government, mainly composed of technocrats, intended to reassure the EU partners of Italian respect for the Economic and Monetary Union (EMU) constraints – particularly inflation, debt-to-GDP ratio and budget deficit.

During the Ciampi government, the electoral law was also modified after the 1993 referendum results (Barbagallo, 2009).[18] Ciampi as PM was also the main player to carry out another tripartite agreement with the cooperation of workers' and employers' organisations. On 23 July 1993, the so-called *Ciampi Protocol* was signed, designed to reform industrial relations and the collective bargaining systems in order to reduce inflation though wage moderation, income policy, investment and productivity increase.

In summary, both Amato and Ciampi as PMs were concerned with the issue of inflation. Both governments decided to overcome the crises by implementing economic and fiscal recovery policies with a profound change in the wage structure and in the industrial relations system (De Luca, 2013) in order to restrict its growth and, at the same time, to establish a concerted economic policy among government and social actors. In any case, from

1992 and 1993, there was little room for budgetary manoeuvre for any Italian Government that aimed to reduce the public debt (Crouch, 2009; Streeck, 2013) and avoid speculative attacks.

Moreover, starting from these two years, technocrats and non-MPs were preferred over politicians to lead Italian Governments, such as Carlo Azeglio Ciampi (1993–94), Lamberto Dini (1995–96) and Mario Monti (2011–13), or to be in charge of the Ministry of Economy and Finance (MEF), of Labour and Social Policies (MLPS), of Economic Development (MISE) and, also, of Education, University and Research (MIUR).

The following section deals with the main measures of economic policy to fight inflation and the debate on this issue within the CGIL.

1.4 The CGIL's positions on the 1992 and 1993 tripartite agreements

In Italy, a long discussion was underway between government, trade unions and employers' organisations about the establishment of a new industrial relations system. Indeed, in the political and economic debate, the central issue is how to contain inflation, and the target became the automatic wage indexation mechanism. It was attacked first by CONFINDUSTRIA in 1982, later reduced by the fifth government led by Amintore Fanfani with the agreement known as *Protocollo Scotti*, signed by his Labour Minister, Vincenzo Scotti, and the workers' and employers' organisations in 1983, and, finally, in 1984 by the first Craxi government.[19]

In the 1990s talks resumed to establish a new kind of industrial relations. A pre-agreement between the seventh Andreotti government and workers' and employers' organisations was signed on 10 December 1991: *Memorandum of understanding for urgent measures to fight inflation* (better known as *Protocollo, 1991*). With this memorandum, the government promoted a proposal for an income policy in order to achieve a structural reduction of the inflation rate over three years (1992–94), the reduction of its differential compared to the other main European countries, the defence of Italy's competitiveness on international markets and, finally, the stability of the Italian lira exchange rate. In the same document, the government made a commitment not to renew or to modify by law the automatic wage indexation mechanism that would expire on 31 December 1991 and to resume the talks on the new bargaining system starting from 1 June 1992 (Protocollo, 1991).

Carrieri (1991) found that the attitude shown by the government and CONFINDUSTRIA during the talks was more inspired by a logic based on short-term maximisation instead of a joint regulation of industrial relations, which required a long-term perspective. The unions were aware of the premature end of the parliamentary mandate and the lack of prestige of the seventh Andreotti Government (Galantini, 1991). Moreover, the intransigence of CONFINDUSTRIA on the automatic wage indexation mechanism – a tool defended in different ways by the unions – reduced the likelihood of concluding the talks with an agreement.

For this reason, the unions proposed to postpone the negotiations over wages and bargaining structure, awaiting the receptiveness of the CONFINDUSTRIA and a more stable political situation. The government undertook not to extend or to modify the automatic wage indexation mechanism, pending the resumption of the tripartite talks. The CGIL General Secretary, Bruno Trentin, said: "We agreed not to request an extension by law, because we believe that the automatic wage indexation mechanism reform must be entrusted to negotiation between the parties" (Sateriale, 1991). Trentin defended his signing of the 1991 Protocol and decided to tackle the internal opposition faction in the CGIL, stressing the challenges inherent to that agreement (Trentin, 1991). Indeed, from the beginning, this matter of modifying of the automatic wage indexation mechanism created a deep disagreement within the CGIL (Agostini, 1992; Alleva, 1992; Sai, 1992).

Actually, the Protocol signed in 1991 seemed more like an agreement to reschedule the core of the talks by the first semester of 1992. This means that to safeguard the wages' purchasing power, a new tool would be created together with an overall reform of the collective bargaining system in the next negotiations. There were different views between government, trade union confederations and industrial employers' organisations, and they remained in their respective positions (Crucianelli, 1992). The CGIL and UIL demanded the payment of the wage increment foreseen in May 1992 (Mascini, 1992) whereas the CISL was immediately willing to negotiate. On the contrary, both the government and CONFINDUSTRIA wanted to move on from the automatic wage indexation mechanism that was scheduled to end on 31 December 1991.

Despite the snap election held in April 1992, at the beginning of June, the government in power was still the same led by PM Andreotti, and the Labour Minister responsible for the tripartite negotiations was Franco Marini. The long-awaited talks opened on 2 June 1992. While the three union confederations had different positions,[20] CONFINDUSTRIA demanded the elimination of any indexation mechanism (Abete, 1996), with wages to be negotiated every two years at sector or plant level and every six years at national level only for the regulatory part, and, finally, they wanted Article 39 of the Italian Constitution to be put into force.[21]

Meanwhile, the talks went ahead, and the new government led by PM Giuliano Amato took office on 28 June 1992. It was therefore Nino Cristofori as the new Labour Minister who coordinated the tripartite talks by encouraging a swift signing of the agreement. On 31 July 1992, the government asked for an immediate conclusion to the talks, failing which the cabinet would present its immediate resignation.

The agreement, called *Protocol on the incomes policy, fight against inflation and labour cost* (better known as *Amato Protocol*), was signed on the same day (Protocollo, 1992). This protocol highlighted the economic and financial risk and the subsequent need to reduce inflation and the public deficit not only to converge towards Maastricht's parameters but also to protect the Italian economic development and to safeguard the citizens' economic security. The Amato Protocol called on the government to implement coherent policies and required appropriate behaviour from the economic and social actors in order to overcome the current difficulties, return to the path of economic development and boost employment. It was thought that all of this would allow Italy to recover its credibility at the international level.

Since the goal was to bring inflation down to 2.0% in three years (1993–1995), the government wanted to keep the wage and labour costs in accordance with the inflation target. All the signatories of this memorandum recognised the firms' need to regain competitiveness and adopted the goal of re-launching employment, in particular in the *Mezzogiorno*. Generally, the 1992 Protocol laid the foundations for an overall income policy, which needed the contribution of all the economic and social actors to work correctly.

Consequently, three decisions were taken: (i) the definitive end of the wage indexation mechanism; (ii) the granting of a lump sum payment of 20,000 Italian lira for 13 months starting from January 1993 to cover the period 1992–1993; (iii) to not bargain for any wages at sector and plant levels.

The following reform of the bargaining system and the wage structure was to be concluded on 15 September 1992. The main guidelines were set: (i) dual bargaining system based on two different, non-overlapping levels; (ii) partial safeguard of workers' purchasing power only during the period between the expired collective bargaining agreement and the new one as an incentive for the parties to negotiate it even with the active role played by government.

The gradual transformation of labour relations within the public administration according to business and private parameters is part of the Amato Protocol. Indeed, the government committed to give public workers the same rights as private ones, also in terms of wage rises.

The government decided to implement the income policy through the following interventions:

1   On prices and tariffs control. The general aim was to contribute to disinflation through monitoring and management tools for public tariffs and self-regulation for free market prices together with the removal of any barriers against an effective competition. As a last resort, in case of speculative prices, the government could have taken prices under its control.

2   On fiscal matters and contributions. The government intended to keep the fiscal pressure constant, on the same conditions as the service offered. For this reason, it proposed the recovery of tax evasion and avoidance, and the fair distribution of fiscal burden among taxpayers.

3   On employment and the labour market. To address the economic and social restructuring more effectively, the government intended to improve social security protections, to create new employment through the introduction of flexibility as other European countries had already done, to incentivise fixed-term hiring and to promote self-employment.

4   On investments. The government proposed to enhance the channelling of resources from savings to investments, to consolidate the role of the stock exchange, to promote pluralism within the financial markets in order to open up additional opportunities for small- and medium-sized enterprises. Moreover, there was a reference for a priority future public investment in innovation and R&D.

Bruno Trentin raised objections to the final text of the tripartite agreement and resigned immediately as CGIL's General Secretary after signing it. In his view, the agreement was in contrast with his mandate received from the CGIL, and he signed just to avoid concrete economic and social crises and to avoid damaging relations with CISL and UIL. As Trentin remembered in his memoirs, this agreement made him fall into depression (Trentin, 2017).

The subsequent tripartite meetings would have discussed the reform of the bargaining structure, indexation for a long period between the expired collective bargaining agreement and the start of the new one, unitary workplace union structure (in Italian *Rappresentanza Sindacale Unitaria* or *RSU*) and income policy. But the harsh budget implemented by the government persuaded the trade unions to call for general strikes in October 1992 and in April 1993.

After the resignation of PM Amato on 21 April 1993, Carlo Azeglio Ciampi took office some days later, on 29 April 1993. Ciampi as PM completed the tripartite agreement with the aim of keeping inflation under control and of modifying industrial relations. Indeed, this agreement – better known as *Ciampi Protocol* – established the reform of the collective bargaining system, of which the main elements were: (i) an income policy system; (ii) a dual bargaining structure based on the national level (industry or specific sectors) and decentralised level (plant or territory); (iii) the setting up of a single workplace union structure at the workplace level (Protocollo, 1993).

1.5 CGIL's economic proposals on development

At the same time, union density continued to decline, and – as will be shown in Chapter 2 – precariousness massively increased. At the beginning of the 2000s, the CGIL reacted to this situation by elaborating an interesting analysis on the causes of Italian economic stagnation. It deserves attention, since this analysis is consistent with that proposed in the following chapters.

Although the CGIL's proposal discussed in this section is outside the period under consideration in the present chapter, it is interesting to re-propose it for the sake of understanding the current economic policy debate in Italy.

On 18 October 2002, the CGIL called a general strike to draw attention specifically to Italy's economic decline and to the need to make radical changes in economic and social policies (Epifani, 2002). This can be considered the starting point in the CGIL's interpretation of the causes and the effects of the Italian economic decline, its active participation in the wider public debate triggered by the Gallino (2003) publication and of its many policy recommendations which later flowed into an overall CGIL's programme (CGIL, 2013).

The starting point of the CGIL's analysis is a critique to the economic policy of Berlusconi's government. Indeed, at the beginning of the 2000s, the second Berlusconi government (2001–2005) promoted some structural reforms with the purpose of boosting growth, with the strong backing of the CONFINDUSTRIA, led by then-president Antonio D'Amato (2000–2004). This development model was essentially based on: (i) less fiscal pressure along with tax amnesties and shields; (ii) increased options for fixed-term labour contracts; (iii) the division of the three largest trade union organisations in order to isolate the CGIL; (iv) the transformation of the public administration according to business parameters; (v) a foreign economic policy based on the support for the exporting of Italian goods.

The demand is for an economic policy able to bring the country out of the decline denounced mainly by the CGIL, which had become a widely recognised issue (Camusso et al., 2003). According to Lapadula (2003), the decline is closely linked with the specialisation of Italian businesses focused on traditional industries and based on under-sized firms. On the other hand, the second Berlusconi government pointed to China as being responsible for Italy's crisis. Indeed, the solution in Lapadula's view is neither duties nor protectionism but a new industrial model able to participate in international trade (Lapadula, 2003).

The seriousness of the Italian situation is continually underlined by the CGIL in labour, fiscal and environmental sectors (Agnello Modica, 2004) but also in the social field (Del Fattore, 2003) and in the institutional one (Troffa, 2004).

The CGIL's critique is regarding the government's choice of an economic development model based on labour costs and on reducing workers' rights. In the CGIL's view, there were many reasons to continue the struggle against the decline (Guzzonato, 2003), especially because the financial and real estate rentiers were promoting wage cuts and penalising investments.

The CGIL's proposals to tackle the economic decline are based on high-quality development, extension of labour rights and on an increased social safety net while at the same time implementing an overall re-thinking of the social model (Rocchi, 2006).

Lapadula (2004) entered the general debate with his book, in which he tracks the historical and economic path of Italian development from the economic miracle until the early 2000s. He believes that it is necessary to make a determined effort to deal with the repositioning of the Italian production specialisation model in order to create value-added goods, given that the traditional Italian price competitiveness, based on low wages and lira devaluation, would be impossible with the euro. In Lapadula's analysis, the main problem is not the euro but the second Berlusconi government's economic policies, which did not tackle the structural problems of the Italian development model, leading to stagnation. Indeed, the policy applied by that government was a neoliberal economic recipe based on reduced taxation, increased labour precariousness, public spending cuts and also on breaking trade union unity.

In contrast, Lapadula considers it necessary to follow a high-quality development model – in order to not be vulnerable to the international lower-quality competition – supported by: (i) more investments in training, research and innovation, which could lead to the growth of productivity, higher work activity rate, larger firm size and recovery of the share in international trade; (ii) the completion of the liberalisation process blocked by corporative interests; (iii) the safeguarding of the social model; (iv) a strong role of the industrial sector; (v) redirection of the largest firms to strengthen the smaller ones and (vi) income policies designed to increase the real wage, raise productivity and distribute income (Lapadula, 2004).

The Italian decline also needs to be tackled through the spread of knowledge (Saltini, 2006). In this way, it would be possible to create jobs, enhance social cohesion and support well-being at all ages. Fammoni (2006) believes that it is also fundamental to deal with unreported employment and the underground economy, which are other Italian structural problems. This is strictly linked with illegality and with the dark side of the current development model, which needs to be fought by the union (Cristilli, 2011).

Moreover, government policies composed of a mixture of liberalism and protectionism will increase the decline, in which the low quality of human capital blocks innovation and, in turn, the low propensity to innovate prevents investment in education and research (Dacrema, 2008).

Indeed, the lack of growth is attributable to the economic thought that inspired the economic policies which were implemented for many years[22] and that did not solve the structural problems behind the Italian economic decline (Beschi and Sanna, 2012).

The CGIL has always formed its own ideas on the reforms needed for the country. In its national congress in 2006, it proposed a new kind of relationship between government and social actors, a different model of development, an innovative economic policy to avoid the two-stage policy (in Italian *politica dei due tempi*) based, first, on rebalancing and, later, on economic growth (CGIL, 2006). In the following national congress in 2010, the CGIL – criticised daily by the fourth Berlusconi government (2008–2011) – called for the return to employer–union dialogue and launched several proposals on economic policies that were never taken into account (CGIL, 2010).

In order to concentrate all the proposals in a strong document, the CGIL drafted its "Program for Jobs"[23] (in Italian *Piano del Lavoro*) during its national conference held in Rome on 25 and 26 January 2013, on the eve of the 2013 general elections. The Program for Jobs – to which different scholars contributed – aims to place the problem of "jobs" and "demand" at the centre of the political dispute. The CGIL believes that it is not possible to have a period of new growth and development without job creation, as it is the only thing that can address the deficiencies of Italian demand and structural weakness (Sanna, 2014).

The serious geographical and intergenerational imbalances, the contraction of employment, the increased inequalities and unemployment affecting the Italian economy were analysed by the CGIL (2013) in a *Keynesian* perspective (lack of aggregate demand, the need to re-establish State intervention in the economy and full employment as the main goal) and some *Schumpeterian* aspects, such as the constant call for innovation (Sanna, 2014; Sateriale, 2013).

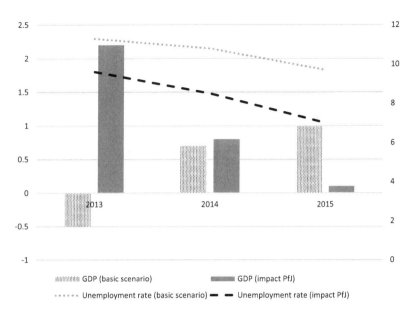

Figure 1.11 GDP (left, %) and unemployment rate (right, %) in the basic scenario
and in the scenario considering the impact of the Program for Jobs (PfJ)

Source: My elaboration on CGIL data (2013)

The Program for Jobs, which starts by examining the aggregate demand
and aims to achieve full employment, contains several proposals in different fields: from labour policies to fiscal ones, from the welfare state to public investments (CGIL, 2013; Giangrande, 2016; Sanna, 2013). The CGIL
harshly criticises the neoliberal agenda implemented in Italy over the past decades through "structural reforms" because they have been completely oriented
to the supply side and to cost competition, making labour appear irrelevant.

The result of the general election and the formation of the Letta government (2013–2014) based on a "great coalition" made the implementation
of the Program for Jobs impossible. It nevertheless remains a detailed plan
deserving attention in view of the economic thought that inspired it, the
concrete proposals drafted, the indication of where the necessary resources
could be found and the potential for a positive impact on the Italian economy.

Indeed, there was also an econometric study made by *Centro Europa
Ricerche* on the Program for Jobs that brought to light the fact that the
impact of the measures envisaged by CGIL represents a strong impetus
to anti-cyclical policies and, in particular, showed that only direct public

intervention would reduce the debt with a simultaneous improvement of GDP growth in the three years considered (2013–2015).

In conclusion, the CGIL maintained that the Italian crisis and the increase of unemployment in the period under consideration is to be imputed to the reduction of public spending (amplified by the massive decrease of public investment) and the measures of labour flexibility. The theoretical basis of the CGIL's interpretation (as well as its policy prescriptions) is *structuralist* in essence, where expansionary fiscal policy is designed to increase both domestic demand (in a short-run perspective) and productivity growth (in a long-run perspective).

Notes

1 It began in the autumn of 1969 and represented the peak of union conflict and social victories on a wide range of claims such as pensions, national minimum wage, housing, transport, health system, education, etc.

2 On 14 October 1980, a demonstration of many thousands of people crossed the centre of Turin. It marked a turning point in the Italian industrial relations history. Indeed, its immediate effect was to put an end to the strike in FIAT – the largest national automotive plant – inducing the trade unions to seek a quick solution for one of the longest industrial disputes.

3 It is the first industrialised region of Italy which began its development between the nineteenth and twentieth centuries. It has been the most productive Italian area based on big Fordist firms, located in the north-west of the country, revolving around Turin, Milan and Genoa. See Felice (2015).

4 Bagnasco (1977) coined this term, inserting it into the traditional Italian division between the north, specifically the north-west, and the *Mezzogiorno*. In his idea, the Third Italy is composed of the north-eastern regions (Emilia-Romagna, Friuli Venezia Giulia, Trentino-Alto Adige and Veneto) and the central regions (Marche, Toscana and Umbria without the Latium). In this area, the dominant mantra was "small is beautiful", and it was characterised by micro and small firms which would also arrive in the Adriatic regions (first in Abruzzo and, later, in Apulia and from there to Basilicata).

5 For the sake of simplicity, this effect rests on the assumption that firms fix prices under the mark-up rule, i.e. they operate in non-perfectly competitive markets. Therefore, when labour productivity grows at a lesser rate than money wages, and prices do not fluctuate, this means that real wages grow at a higher rate than labour productivity.

6 A further argument explaining why as wages increase so does labour productivity is related to the increasing division of labour, according to what is called the Smith effect.

7 However, international trade will not be the focus of this book.

8 The mainstream view supports the idea that when the individual worker chooses to join the trade union, they are maximising a utility function which includes the expected benefits deriving from union action. Unions are assumed to be monopsonist in the labour market and to maximise the benefits of their members. In the standard neoclassical model, insofar as union action generates wage rises, and given the inverse relation between the unitary real wage and employment,

union action eventually causes involuntary unemployment. Moreover, insofar as higher money wages generate inflationary pressures, union action is supposed to redistribute income at the expense of the employed via the decline of their real incomes. On the basis of this theoretical framework, the dramatic decline of union density in most OECD countries appears difficult to explain. Checchi and Visser (2005) refer to compositional change in functional income distribution, linking it to increasing risk aversion on the part of workers.

9 The bombing that killed 17 people and wounded other 88 in Fontana Square in Milan on 12 December 1969 represents the beginning of the so-called "strategy of tension". According to Foa (1996), the bombing was a warning to the labour movement that if workers and unions continued with their social claims, a prompt reaction through disorder, violence and fascism was ready.

10 In recent times, many models of business cycles have been proposed that included, among others, elements of Keynes and Kalecki's thought. Colacchio (2014) summarised those models and pointed out that the "history of agents – and then their memory – strongly affects their current behavior".

11 For a detailed history of European monetary integration from the EMS to the EMU, see Gros and Thygesen (1992) and Fauri (2006).

12 BOT stands for "*Buono Ordinario del Tesoro*", that is, Italy's ordinary Treasury bill. For a historical portrait of the Italian population's saving abilities, see Aresu (2017).

13 For a supplementary economic and political history of the European Union, see Morata (1999), Mammarella and Cacace (2013).

14 This literally means "clean hands". It was the main judicial investigation against corruption led by the public prosecutor Antonio Di Pietro. Thousands of politicians, leaders of the mainstream political parties, public servants, businessmen, bankers, were charged and convicted. For more detailed information, see both historical analysis (Barbagallo, 2009) and journalistic reconstruction (Barbacetto et al., 2012).

15 The general elections held on 5 and 6 April 1992 caused a "political earthquake" (Lepre, 2006). Indeed, the main government parties like the DC and the PSI lost votes together with the new parties that had evolved from the Italian Communist Party (PCI), namely the Democratic Party of the Left (PDS) and Communist Refoundation Party (PRC). The winner of the 1992 elections was the Northern League (LN), a right-wing regionalist party. The so-called "First Republic", was over and a new long transition path started at that moment (Galli, 2004).

16 The public prosecutors Giovanni Falcone and Paolo Borsellino were assassinated by the mafia in Sicily. The first was killed in a bomb attack on the A29 motorway near the town of Capaci on 23 May 1992; the latter died due to a car bomb in Palermo on 19 July 1992.

17 For more details on wage moderation in the 1970s in Italy, it is worth mentioning the debate between Franco Modigliani and Augusto Graziani analysed by Colacchio and Forges Davanzati (2019a). Modigliani blamed high real wages for the decrease of economic growth and the increase in the dualist contrast inside the labour market between over-protected workers and unemployed workers. In contrast, Graziani criticised this hypothesis – based on the inverse correlation between wages and employment – and pointed out that wages are determined by the firms' and workers' bargaining power and, therefore, by the conflict over income distribution.

18 In Italy, pure proportional representation had been in force since 1946. Since 1993, the Italian electoral system has been reformed four times combining all types of electoral methods: (i) the *Mattarellum* used in 1994, 1996 and 2001 general elections; (ii) the *Porcellum* used in 2006, 2008 and 2013 general elections; (iii) the *Italicum* has never been used because the constitutional court judged it partly unconstitutional; (iii) the *Rosatellum* used in the 2018 general election. It is worth saying that the aim of all these electoral reforms has been to guarantee governability and make voters feel closer to their MPs. However, according to the data provided by Italy's Interior Ministry, the outcome has been a continuous decrease of voter turnout (Ministero dell'Interno, 2019). Streeck (2013) gives an interesting insight into the decline of political participation in the OECD countries and the increase in public debt.

19 This government decision divided the trade union movement: on one side, CISL, UIL and the socialist wing of CGIL were in favour and, on the other side the communist wing of CGIL was against it. This led to the dissolution of the Unitary Federation CGIL–CISL–UIL (1972–1984) and opened a phase of reduction of the conflict in the Italian trade union movement.

20 The CGIL did not give up an automatic mechanism to protect the workers' purchasing power and for this reason put forward a proposal based on a two-level bargaining system (national and decentralised) and two wage increments per year fixed according the expected inflation, along with a possible realignment process once a year just in case of deviation between the effective and the targeted inflation levels. The CISL was willing to stop the automatic wage indexation mechanism only if the decentralised bargaining system was sure. The UIL wanted to centralise wage dynamics, limiting its growth to the annually targeted inflation.

21 The article states that

> Trade unions may be freely established. No obligations may be imposed on trade unions other than registration at local or central offices, according to the provisions of the law. A condition for registration is that the statutes of the trade unions establish their internal organisation on a democratic basis. Registered trade unions are legal persons. They may, through a unified representation that is proportional to their membership, enter into collective labour agreements that have a mandatory effect for all persons belonging to the categories referred to in the agreement.

22 After the 2006 General Elections, Romano Prodi was appointed PM, supported by a centre-left coalition. Fausto Bertinotti, former member of the national board of the CGIL, and Franco Marini, former general secretary of the CISL and former Labour Minister, were elected, respectively, as speakers of the Chamber of Deputies and the Senate. Moreover, the Minister of Labour of the second Prodi government was Cesare Damiano, former national vice-secretary of the CGIL's metal workers' union federation (FIOM). Despite the top positions of people from the trade union movement in the government and in the Parliament, the labour policy did not change.

23 Official translation used by the CGIL.

2 Labour market flexibilisation and the decentralised bargaining system

2.1 Introduction

The successful attack on the Italian unions – as shown in the previous chapter – allowed Italian business organisations to demand government policies of labour market deregulation as well intervention designed to reduce the workers' bargaining power, such as decentralised wage bargaining. In this chapter, I will consider labour flexibility as a range of economic policy measures devoted to changing labour contracts towards non-standard forms of employment, deregulating the institutional set-up and to modifying the standard industrial relations which regulate it. I will focus on two main aspects of labour flexibility: the deregulation of labour contracts – reflected in the path of Employment Protection Legislation (EPL) as elaborated by the OECD – and the shift from centralised collective bargaining to a decentralised form.

These economic policy measures were implemented assuming the theoretical framework of the neoclassical synthesis, where it is assumed that unemployment is ultimately caused by real wage rigidity, and real wage rigidity is assumed to be endogenous, depending on the mutual agreement between workers and employers to settle the wage unit at a level higher than that of equilibrium.

The rationale for these measures can be traced in the attempt to make Italian firms more price-competitive, by means of fiscal measures, monetary policies and exchange agreements that have systematically enabled them to compete by cutting wages. Policies of labour market deregulation were consistent with this view: insofar as they generated wage moderation and, hence, deflation, they put Italian firms in a position to compete by cutting prices. The reduction of prices of exported goods was expected to increase aggregate demand and, as a result, the rate of growth. Moreover, the decline of wages is supposed to reduce imports via the reduction of consumption. At the same time, proponents of these measures supported the view that

DOI: 10.4324/9781003089322-3

labour market deregulation was a necessary device in order to increase the employment level (Layard et al., 1991).

Accordingly, the struggle over income distribution in the 1970s can be conceived as the struggle between two radically different ideas on the way to stimulate economic growth: a wage-led model, combined with increasing public investment, supported by the CGIL, *versus* profit-led and an export-led models – driven by the reduction of wages – supported by CONFINDUSTRIA. This chapter aims at providing (i) a historical reconstruction of the "reforms" of the labour market institutions (1997–2003) and a reconstruction of the main arguments on the supposed positive effects of labour market deregulation on employment; (ii) a theoretical and empirical assessment of the effects of labour market deregulation on aggregate demand, labour productivity growth and the fluctuations of employment rates. The concluding section of this chapter deals with the effects of decentralised collective bargaining on wages and on the rate of growth of labour productivity.

I will analyse the impact of labour market reforms on the unemployment rate and the labour productivity rate, emphasising the gap between the desired outcomes (i.e. increasing employment and productivity) and the real outcomes.

The exposition is organised as follows. Section 2.2 deals with alarmism on labour market rigidity and the debate on the reforms of the labour market in Italy in the period between 1997 and 2013, considering the EPL index provided by the OECD as the main indicator of labour market flexibility. Section 2.3 deals with decentralised collective bargaining, and Section 2.4 concludes the chapter.

2.2 The alarmism on labour market rigidity: the academic debate and the reforms

Policies of labour market deregulation in Italy were supported by a cultural climate which posed *the alarmism on labour market rigidity*. This alarmism was theorised by the seminal book by Layard et al. (1991) with reference to so-called *"Eurosclerosis"*, based on the idea that the labour market in Europe had too many rigidities in the minimum wage level and in the firm's freedom to hire and fire workers in comparison with the labour market in the United States of America (Blanchard, 2007). This argument was used to justify labour market reforms across the EU, though with different intensity and depth among the EU countries.

In Italian academic circles, this alarmism translated into a widespread consensus on the necessity to overcome the traditional way of implementing industrial relations. In the economic policy field, the Italian lawmakers

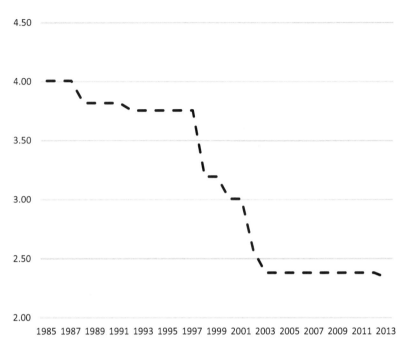

Figure 2.1 EPL in Italy (1985–2013)
Source: My elaboration on OECD data

of the period under consideration implemented measures of labour market deregulation which were more intense and faster than other European countries (Lampa and Perri, 2014).

Labour market flexibilisation was implemented successfully through three main reforms[1] that increased firms' freedom in hiring and firing workers, designed to prevent workers from achieving higher wages: (i) the Treu Package (Law no. 196/1997) introduced the new fixed-term contracts; (ii) the fixed-term contract reform (Legislative Decree no. 368/2001) eliminated the limits on the exceptional nature of temporary contracts; (iii) the Biagi Reform (Law no. 30/2003) introduces dozens of new fixed-term contracts, which expanded the possibilities of hiring workers on non-standard contracts.

Conventionally, economists use the EPL index to measure the degree of labour flexibility.[2] Figure 2.1 shows the decline of the EPL from 1985 to 2013, which occurred mainly between 1997 and 2003, after the aforementioned reforms.

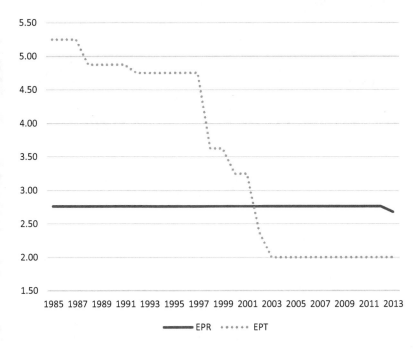

Figure 2.2 EPR and EPT in Italy (1985–2013)
Source: My elaboration on OECD data

The drop of the EPL is due to the collapse of only one of its indexes. Indeed, as we can see, the EPR, which is the indicator that measures the strictness of regulation of individual dismissal of employees on regular/ indefinite contracts, remained unchanged at 2.76 for the entire period considered, falling to 2.68 in 2013 after the reform implemented in 2012. The EPT, which is the indicator for temporary employment that measures the strictness of regulation on the use of fixed-term and temporary work agency contracts, plummeted from 5.25 in 1985 to 2.00 in 2013. The collapse occurred right after the 1997 reform, which introduced new fixed-term contracts, and the 2001 reform, which eliminated the justification required from employers opting for temporary contracts instead of permanent positions.

The widespread consensus in Italian political circles on the necessity to reduce employment protection reflected a common belief among economists on the view that labour market deregulation promotes increasing employment and economic growth.

The fundamental arguments in this theoretical framework were the following:

1 *Expected costs of firing activities.* As labour contracts become less "rigid", implying that firms are able to fire with low costs, it is assumed that their expectations on future profits increase. This, in turn, would produce an increase in investment and employment. In other words, labour flexibility, as regards labour contracts, is seen as a precondition for the increase of the employment rate (Forges Davanzati and Mongelli, 2018).

2 *Profit-led model.* Wage moderation, which is the effect of the workers' decreasing bargaining power due to labour market deregulation policies, re-distributes income to the benefit of firms. On the assumption that investments are also financed via internal funds, this would produce an increase in private investment and the consequent increase in the employment rate. This is a case where economic growth is driven by capital accumulation, in a profit-led regime (Bhaduri and Marglin, 1990; Hein, 2017).

3 *Export-led model.* Moreover, as wage moderation produces deflation, it is considered an effective strategy in order to increase exports and reduce imports. In this case, economic growth (and the increase in the employment rate) is driven by net exports. This is the case of a growth model based on a "neo-mercantilist" regime. Despite the fact that this mainstream economic model growth presents evident limitations (Ostry et al., 2016), it is still the reference model within the EU.

4 *Shirker model.* On the assumption that workers do not get intrinsic satisfaction from their job, the increased uncertainty about the renewal of their labour contract is expected to stimulate their effort (Shapiro and Stiglitz, 1984). The consequent increase in labour productivity would produce economic growth and a higher employment rate.

Since the 1980s, the debate has revolved around the incentive to work and the role of unemployment. Among different opinions, it is important to mention the study of the threat of firing workers as a disciplinary device (Calvo, 1981). The mainstream approach, in its different visions, is based on the idea that the real wage and the level of employment are negatively correlated. Accordingly, the level of employment can increase only if the real wage unit decreases.

Within the mainstream approach, the efficiency wage theory should be considered. This stresses the fact that labour productivity growth is driven by individual effort while capital accumulation is less important. Workers

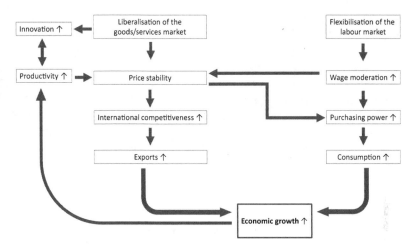

Figure 2.3 Purpose of structural reforms in goods/services and labour markets

Source: My own elaboration based on Tronti (2009) model

are regarded as people who naturally tend to shirk and the unemployment benefit as a tool that attenuates the threat of being laid off. According to this view, unemployment is the natural outcome of wage rises spontaneously given by firms to their employees in order to stimulate their effort. The macro result is involuntary unemployment, confirming the inverse relationship between the real wage and the level of employment. In terms of policy proposals, it is suggested that welfare benefits should be reduced in order to prevent workers from shirking.

In the last few decades, this intensive economic debate has supported flexibility in the labour market in order to increase growth and employment and has subsequently promoted so-called structural labour market reforms (Brancaccio et al., 2018). Many OECD countries – specifically those in the EU – have prevailed in the overall deregulation of their labour markets.

According to the dominant view, the deregulation of the labour market should be the way to allocate workers quickly to respond to firms' needs. Moreover, wage moderation should be the precondition to keep prices stable, in order to increase workers' purchasing power and firms' competitiveness, assuming a simultaneous labour market flexibilisation and liberalisation in the markets for goods and services. The final goal should have been to generate growth through the increase in exports (Blanchard and Giavazzi, 2003).

As we have seen in the previous chapter, the workers paid the cost of inflation reduction (Tridico, 2015; Tronti, 2005). In particular, the "*masochistic political exchange*" (Tronti, 2009) – that is wage reduction combined with the increase of private investments – occurred only to the detriment of their purchasing power insofar as firms did not react to wage decreases by investing more (which may be due to the deterioration of firms' expectations). Hence, this wage moderation policy has negatively affected the wages and workers' purchasing power because it was acting in a framework with a lack of private investments. It then led to the decrease of consumption and, consequently, of aggregate demand (Forges Davanzati et al., 2017; Tridico, 2014a; Tronti, 2010). Moreover, the drop has been even more significant because there was an incomplete reform of the social protection system (Leonardi, 2009) such as unemployment benefit and its payees.

First, the Italian lawmakers aimed to respect the Maastricht economic parameters, thus reducing public spending to the detriment of wages as mentioned in the previous chapter. Second, they have implemented only one side of the *flexicurity* model promoted by the EU with European Employment Strategy (1997) and later with the Lisbon Strategy (2000), following Northern European best practices. Therefore, Italy has strongly implemented *flexibility* in its national employment legislation without adopting *security*,[3] an aspect which has seen only some minor occasional reforms.

The realisation of these measures has had a negative impact in Italy, above all because of the Italian production structure and its productivity. It should be pointed out that the Italian enterprises are small-sized, lack competitiveness, are quite often family-owned and are mainly active in the domestic market (ISTAT, 2014; Trésor-Economics, 2016). Moreover, most of the Italian firms have this kind of production specialisation in low technology-intensive sectors, above all in the *Mezzogiorno* (Bronzini et al., 2013).

It is worth highlighting that the reforms mentioned earlier – wage indexation elimination, promotion of the decentralised bargaining system and labour market flexibilisation – were negotiated in a tripartite way, or indirectly accepted by the largest trade union confederations – sometimes with the opposition of CGIL.

In the next section, I will deal with the empirical and theoretical link between wages and employment, assuming that – as shown in this section – a decline of the EPL, combined with the continuously rising unemployment rate and labour precariousness, makes wages fall.

2.3 The effects of labour market deregulation on employment and labour productivity

Evidence from the ISTAT seems to contradict the mainstream view, at least in the Italian case and at least in the period under consideration.

Figures 2.4 and 2.5 can be explained by considering the increase of non-standard jobs and labour precariousness. In other words, while the employment rate increases, it seems that quality, hours worked and wages of the new jobs decrease. The decline of wages involves a deterioration of the quality of the workforce, being associated with lower education, which, in a long-run perspective, reduces the growth of labour productivity (Forges Davanzati and Giangrande, 2019c). This is a problem of lack of co-ordination: the individual firm finds it convenient to cut wages, while at the aggregate level and in a long-run perspective, this produced

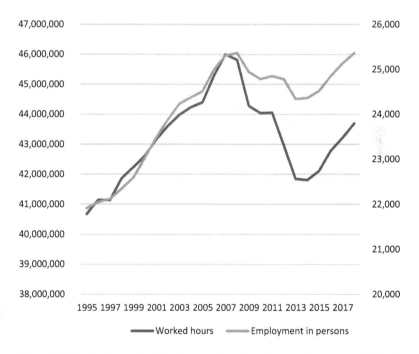

Figure 2.4 Worked hours (left, in thousands) and employment in persons (right, in thousands) (1995–2017)

Source: My elaboration on ISTAT data

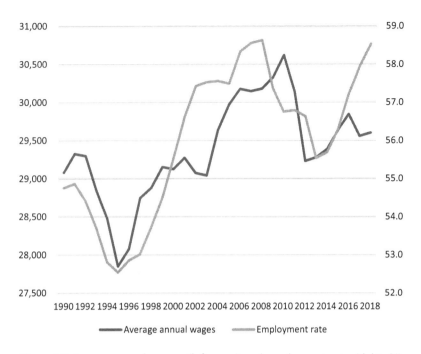

Figure 2.5 Average annual wages (left, euro) and employment rate (right, %) (1990–2018)

Source: My elaboration on OECD and ISTAT data

a decline of labour productivity growth and of profits at the expense of firms as a whole.

The result of these labour reforms has been the creation of many economic areas excluded from national and collective bargaining. The claim of mainstream scholars that are still stressing that labour productivity in Italy is lower than in other EU countries because of the excessive protection of employment appears questionable. Indeed, Italy has reduced its EPL index faster and more thoroughly than other OECD countries (Forges Davanzati and Mongelli, 2018; Perri and Lampa, 2018).

These arguments are in line with Paolo Sylos Labini's view (1984) that the path of labour productivity depends on the wages to profits ratio (which Sylos Labini labels the Ricardo effect) and on aggregate demand (which is labelled as the Smith effect).

Figures 2.6 and 2.7 show the links between labour market flexibility and the employment rate and the unemployment rate.[4] There are several

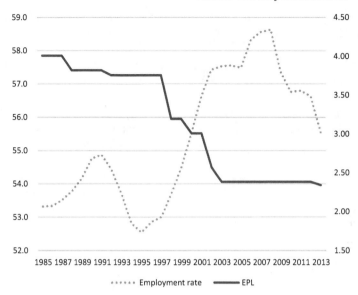

Figure 2.6 Employment rate (left, %) and EPL (right, index) (1985–2013)
Source: My elaboration on ISTAT and OECD data

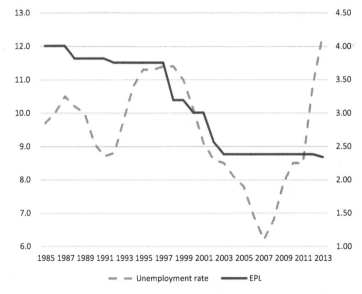

Figure 2.7 Unemployment rate (left, %) and EPL (right, index) (1985–2013)
Source: My elaboration on ISTAT and OECD data

theoretical arguments supporting the view that a policy of wage moderation negatively affects both employment and unemployment:

1   Policies of labour market deregulation reduce the labour share and, hence, consumption and domestic demand. This effect is amplified by the decline of the propensity to consume due to the increasing uncertainty connected with the renewal of the labour contract (Pacella, 2008). The decline of consumption is due to the increasing uncertainty on the part of workers about the renewal of their labour contract (Stockhammer and Ramskogler, 2008).

2   Such policies encourage firms to compete via wage cutting, reducing their propensity to innovate. In other words, the drop in labour productivity, which occurred in Italy starting from the early 1990s, can also be explained by considering the fact that wage moderation acted as a disincentive to invest in innovation (Kleinknecht, 2015). Indeed, when employment increases, firms find it hard to reduce wages, and they are forced to innovate (Dutt, 2012).

3   Wage moderation is a cause of deflation. Deflation, in turn, reduces current consumption and current private investment, thus depressing domestic demand and pushing up the unemployment rate (Storm, 2019b).[5]

4   Moreover, if a link between wages and labour productivity exists, wage moderation produces deterioration of the quality of the workforce, being associated with lower education and poorer nutrition, which, in a long-run perspective, reduces the rate of growth of labour productivity (Forges Davanzati and Giangrande, 2019c).

5   Wage moderation is likely not to increase net exports. This may occur in countries where exports are mainly driven by non-price competitiveness and, in the Italian case, evidence seems to support this effect (Felettigh and Federico, 2011; Paternesi Meloni, 2018).[6]

A more general remark is in order. As emphasised by McCombie and Thirlwall (1994), while economic growth can be export-led, the opposite link may occur, meaning that as an economy grows and labour productivity rises, this generates a decline of the unit labour cost and the consequent decrease of prices. Provided that exports are sensitive to prices (and this is not the Italian case, at least in the period under consideration and for most of its exports), economic growth is a pre-condition for increasing exports, giving rise to a virtuous circle of increasing economic growth, increasing exports, increasing aggregate demand and employment rate.

Finally, one can consider the fact that as wages decline, the consequent deflation contributes to a deflationary path. Deflation then causes an increase of the real interest rates on public debt. In an institutional context, where it is not profitable for a government to tax the banking sector (being the owner of State bonds) or firms (particularly firms mobile on the international plane), most of the taxation is levied on labour. This reduces the net disposable income for low-income households, giving rise to a vicious circle of low wages, low productivity growth, high public debt and high unemployment – that is the so-called debt-deflation effect (Fisher, 1933).

Perhaps worse, wage moderation contributes to a change in the consumption structure, which has increased, in turn, the importing of all those goods no longer produced in the country. Leon (2008) criticised Friedman's *permanent income* and Modigliani's *life cycle hypothesis*, both of which ignored the relationship between consumption and income, therefore ousting the *Keynesian multiplier* from economic theory and paving the way to the lack of economic pluralism (Bellofiore, 2018b).

In line with the theoretical framework adopted here, one can motivate the repetition of this line of economic policy following Kalecki's view that capitalists are against the full employment policy because dismissal would cease to be a disciplinary measure. Indeed, in a full employment economy, the social strength of business would be weakened by the workers' stronger bargaining power, which could allow them to call for strikes for higher wages and improvements in working conditions. In this framework, workers' class-consciousness would increase, and it could cause deep social and economic changes, with more power in the political sphere. Hence, entrepreneurs prefer to keep unemployment as a means to discipline workers' claims and instead welcome increased stability at the political level more than higher profits, as clarified in his *Political Aspects of Full Employment* (Kalecki, 1943).

In a capitalist economy, the role of trade unions is essential. Indeed, the union struggle can achieve wage rises, restrain the mark-up fixed by firms and modify income distribution from profits to wages, but only if there is an excess of capacity. Conversely, a wage drop tends to weaken the unions' bargaining power and leads to a fall in employment. Hence, the unions' bargaining activity can codetermine the distribution of national income. According to Kalecki, there are other forms of class struggle than wage bargaining, as explained in his *Class Struggle and the Distribution of National Income* (1971). Indeed, another way to influence income distribution and favour workers is price control or, alternatively, the subsiding of the price of wage goods by taxing profits (Kalecki, 1971).

According to Nicholas Kaldor, wage rises can positively affect labour productivity. Evidence shows that in countries where the wages are higher, the labour productivity is also higher (OECD, 2017). Since the union density within big firms in the manufacturing sector is higher than in smaller firms and other sectors (Kaldor, 1989) the bigger ones not only have higher internal resources but, also under union pressure, may pay higher wages to their employees. Big firms can pay higher wages to their workers not only because of the efficiency wage theory but also to gain good labour relations (Colacchio and Forges Davanzati, 2017).

Hence, in this Kaleckian and Kaldorian framework, the result of wage moderation combined with fiscal consolidation is the following. These policies trigger the reduction of aggregate demand via consumption and public expenditure, which leads to the increase of unemployment, the reduction of wages, the further drop of consumption, the fall of profits for firms active in the domestic market and the reduction of public and private investments. In conclusion, the collapse of labour productivity leads to a low, or negative, growth rate.

This can be regarded as an augmented version of the Paolo Sylos Labini productivity function, where the productivity growth depends on the Smith effect (i.e. the increase of demand pushes the increase of productivity) and the Ricardo effect (i.e. the increase in the wage-rate to rate of profit ratio pushes the increase of productivity) (Sylos Labini, 1984). Indeed, it expands the Sylos Labini function insofar as it provides a link between the rate of unemployment and productivity growth, where both are taken into account. Hence, I can deem that higher union density leads to strong union conflict, which drives wage increases. This, in turn, increases the labour productivity, which boosts the growth rate.

Moreover, Perri and Lampa (2017) identified the income distribution deterioration as the cause of the economic crisis. According to their vision, the latter led to a reduction of aggregate demand and of innovative investments, and wage moderation also acted as a disincentive to invest, determining a labour productivity drop (Perri and Lampa, 2018).

Following Kalecki, I can deem the increase in unemployment and the decrease of union density to lead to the reduction of the unions' bargaining power in the economic field, which means less representation of workers' interests in the political arena. This leads to the reduction of public spending on welfare, which in turn increases unemployment and, consequently, reduces labour productivity in a mechanism of CCC, in the mode of Kaldor (1966).[7]

Finally, wage moderation also affects the degree of unused capital. In fact, as wages decline, firms tend to try to stay competitive via the reduction of their costs, which involves less expenditure for fixed capital. If – as in the Italian case – they work with unused capital, wage moderation acts as an incentive not to exploit it (Lavoie, 2014).

2.4 The effects of decentralised wage bargaining on wages and labour productivity

In the academic debate, there was broad consensus that labour flexibility policies are effective for increasing employment and economic growth, especially during the period from the 1980s to the first decade of the 2000s (Layard et al., 1991).

The promoters of so-called active labour market policies shifted the focus to other forms of flexibility: to wage and contractual flexibility. The focus was on the redefinition of Italian industrial relations and favoured decentralised collective bargaining at plant or territorial level.

It should also be noted that historically the "internal flexibility" allowed to firms preceded the "external" flexibility. In the Italian case, this means that wage and organisational flexibility measures – which lead to job precariousness and the growth of undeclared work – are put into effect through the decentralisation of production as a capitalist reaction to the cycle of workers' struggles in 1970s (Moro, 2015). The subsequent policy – which was to be implemented from the 1990s – consisted in allowing firms more "external" flexibility, which meant flexibility in both hiring and dismissal in order to bring the undeclared workers to light.

In any case, it is worth mentioning that in Italy decentralised collective bargaining is still very secondary due to the lack of unions within micro- and small-sized firms, which are 95.2% of the Italian firms (ISTAT, 2014; Ricci and Tronti, 2018).

The interpretation that will be proposed here is based on the conviction that the measures to strengthen decentralised collective bargaining are part of the labour market deregulation process begun in 1993 with the *Ciampi Protocol* and boosted since 2009. Moreover, the theoretical framework behind these policies can be subjected to radical criticism in their logical structure as well as with reference to the gap between expected results and results obtained.

Nevertheless, it is important to mention that under the given conditions (i.e. union presence in all plants and production structure based on larger firms), decentralised bargaining can contribute to generating positive macroeconomic effects, as regards wages and labour productivity growth. I believe that the establishment of decentralised bargaining is a pillar of the wage moderation policy and that on the theoretical level this policy is motivated by the firms' need to link wage dynamics to labour productivity.

This section will show the evolution of decentralised bargaining, providing an overall picture of the CGIL positions and the theoretical framework.

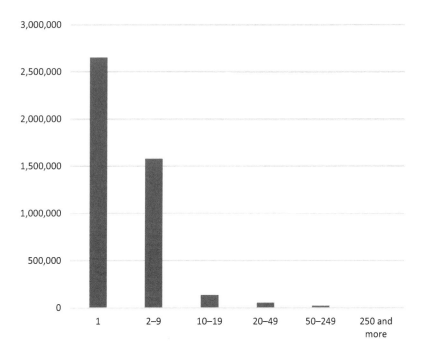

Figure 2.8 Total firm size by persons employed (2012)
Source: My elaboration on ISTAT data

The agreement of 22 January 2009, signed between the government and the social actors – without the CGIL – replaced the 1993 Protocol and represented the risk of strengthening corporate power within firms (Zoppoli, 2011).

It is worth saying that the relationship between the National Collective Bargaining Agreement (in Italian *Contratto Collettivo Nazionale di Lavoro* or CCNL) and second-level bargaining within firms has always been a source of conflict between the unions, in particular between CGIL and CISL. This contrast is the result of two completely different conceptions of union representation: indeed, the CGIL is more attentive to the general representation of workers while the CISL emphasises the membership aspect.[8]

Later, on 28 June 2011, the agreement signed between CONFINDUSTRIA, CGIL, CISL and UIL established the common aim to develop the decentralised bargaining system without prejudice to the CCNL role. The second-level agreements are valid only if approved by the majority of the members of the RSU. Moreover, the organisations' signatories agreed that industrial relations and bargaining matters are entrusted to the autonomous decision of the parties.

A few weeks later, however, in the summer of 2011, Article no. 8 of Law no. 148/2011 was issued: "Support for local collective bargaining". This article, with a fairly ambiguous title, introduced the chance for the workers' organisations or their union representatives to sign agreements at plant and territorial levels, notwithstanding the CCNL, with application to all workers if signed on a majority basis. This legislative intervention – officially not requested by any of the social partners and that recalls the Saint Valentine's decree in 1984 – represented government interference in a system of industrial relations that had been rebuilt after many difficulties. Indeed, this government intrusion[9] undermined an agreement reached after years of severe tension thanks to the autonomous initiative of the largest trade union confederations and the largest employers' organisation (Leonardi et al., 2017). Article 8 issued by the Italian Government with the aim of boosting productivity in fact represents governmental interference – influenced by the maximum monetary authority at European level – in order to dismantle the role of CCNL.

Later, the Monti government (2011–2013) also proposed and signed on 16 November 2012 an agreement with the social partners – without the CGIL – with the aim of boosting the growth of productivity and competitiveness. This agreement proposed stable tax breaks on the so-called "productivity wage" that could be connected – through decentralised bargaining – to the firm's productivity goals.

As already seen, the CGIL launched the Program for Jobs with the aim of full employment through a decent, contracted and paid job with universal and specific forms of protection. In the Program for Jobs, the two-level system is reiterated: (i) the CCNL defines in general, the protections, rights, purchasing power, all labour relations and (ii) decentralised bargaining implements those matters delegated by the CCNL in the field of work organisation, professionalism and wage growth.

Social and territorial bargaining, together with trade union dialogue with the regional and municipal governments, can represent the moment of implementation and verification of the Program for Jobs, which can contribute to a more equitable use of resources – especially in a time of crisis of local finances. Finally, it can become the tool for the diffusion of a homogeneous local welfare to the whole country (CGIL, 2013).

The Program for Jobs also hoped that firms would consider it indispensable to increase investment in research, to enhance work, to implement both process and product innovations and, finally, to encourage larger-sized firms and grouping of enterprises with the dual aim of strengthening their ability to respond to the international competition and, simultaneously, to generate more growth for Italy (Forges Davanzati and Giangrande, 2019d).

The result of the 2013 general elections, and the formation of a "great coalition" government led by Enrico Letta, made the implementation of the Program for Jobs impractical. Nevertheless, it remains an overall project that deserves attention for the economic thought that inspired it, for the depth of the proposals, for the indication of the necessary resources and, finally, for the expected impact on the Italian economy (Giangrande, 2016).

The memorandum of understanding signed on 31 May 2013 between CONFINDUSTRIA, CGIL, CISL and UIL was a follow-up to the previous 2011 agreement and established the principles of the measure of representativeness and bargaining power. In trade union matters, these two themes – representativeness and bargaining – go hand in hand with: (i) who and how many are represented and (ii) what is contracted and where (Forges Davanzati and Giangrande, 2017a).

Is important to underline the fact that a significant proportion of firms, even among those that already have decentralised bargaining, declared their dissatisfaction with the current bargaining system (D'Amuri and Giorgiantonio, 2015). Inconsistencies and regulatory uncertainties may hinder the use of decentralised bargaining to modify and adapt to the plant-level context what is established at national level. Indeed, these critical issues may have reduced the effectiveness of incentives to productivity wages, limiting – or complicating – the possibility of obtaining process innovations using wage leverage.

The ineffectiveness of decentralised bargaining is manifested not only through the dissatisfaction of firms, but also, and above all, through the dissatisfaction of workers, who see their bargaining power and wages reduced.

On this, the analysis proposed by Calmfors and Driffill (1988) is relevant to the role of union bargaining power in determining the results of wage negotiation. The power of the union is directly proportional to the level of centralisation; in fact, as the level of centralisation increases unions acquire market power and greater capacity to influence wages. However, at the same time, wage bargaining has a greater impact on the level of consumer prices, and it therefore leads to the moderation of wage claims.

In contrast, with full decentralisation, the unions have no market power, as demanding a higher wage than other firms in the same sector would lead to a sharp drop in demand and therefore in employment for their own firm.

This would lead to wage moderation and a return to higher employment. In other words, a trade-off emerges between the unions' market power and the impact of wages on prices. The analysis of Calmfors and Driffill (1988) not only investigates the effects of centralised or decentralised bargaining but also forms of intermediate centralisation.

According to the authors, the latter are associated with higher wages and lower employment levels. This would happen because, if the unions are able to influence bargaining in a whole sector, and the goods produced by the different sectors are imperfect substitutes, it would be possible to increase real wages in a particular area, which would not be transmitted fully on the general price level (D'Amuri and Giorgiantonio, 2015).

However, it should be considered that the analysis by Calmfors and Driffill (1988) was carried out in a different context from the current deflationary phase and that, therefore, in the given conditions there is no expectation – even if it is a desirable effect – of an increase in the inflation rate deriving from the wage rise in a highly concentrated bargaining system.

In addition, there is evidence that the growth of union bargaining power, in a centralised bargaining system, tends to be associated with more employment (Flanagan, 1999). There is also an important link between bargaining at the firm level and wage dispersion within firms.

Checchi and Pagani (2005), on this point, found that Italian firms covered by second-level bargaining are characterised by less internal wage dispersion. Finally, Dell'Aringa and Pagani (2007) empirically pointed out that in countries that have two levels of bargaining, there is no greater wage dispersion in firms with second-level bargaining; instead, where second-level bargaining can replace sectoral bargaining, this can be linked to wage dispersion.

Flanagan (1999) pointed out that strongly centralised bargaining tends to be associated with low real wages due to the inflationary effects generated by high nominal wages in centralised bargaining. It should be noticed that decentralised bargaining tends to generate low rates of labour productivity growth but higher employment, since it allows the survival of firms destined to fail in a centralised bargaining structure (the so-called trade-off between productivity and employment).

From the empirical evidence, it can be seen that the decentralised bargaining system is not always associated with a reduction of workers' bargaining power, wages and labour productivity. On this point, it should be noticed that in Northern Italian firms, second-level bargaining is relatively more widespread. Some of these firms do not consider themselves satisfied with the decentralised bargaining system, since it reduces labour productivity and, consequently, profits. Other firms express satisfaction because at the firm level second-level bargaining may fill some gaps that could occur at national level.

More specifically, firms found it convenient to adapt what has been established at the national level to their own context through a decentralised bargaining structure. Furthermore, the productivity bonuses granted to workers at the firm level served as an incentive to productivity, and as a result, overall second-level bargaining – although with some exceptions – was adopted by Northern Italian firms and did not significantly reduce the bargaining power of workers.

It must be specified that second-level wage bargaining can be applied where the production context and the nature of the firms allow it. Since in Italy there is a strong regional gap between north and south, particularly with regard to the production structure, decentralised bargaining may not have the same results that occurred in Northern Italian firms. This happens because the firms in the *Mezzogiorno* are of micro and small size, with a low propensity for innovation, and are composed of a lower number of employees compared to northern firms. The effects of decentralised bargaining therefore depend on the firm's production structure and on the regional production fabric in which it is located.

Second-level bargaining could therefore prove to be unsuccessful in micro and small-sized firms in Southern Italy, and this could increasingly diminish the bargaining power of workers. In this perspective, the way the wage is negotiated must be adapted to suit the local situation, given the heterogeneity of the firms present in the Italian territory.

For example, it is obvious that a decentralised bargaining system can decrease the bargaining power of the workers in a firm with few employees, who are not members of a union. This happens because, given a structural asymmetry between the employer and workers, a decentralised bargaining system would pursue the interests of the employer who, in order to obtain higher profits, pushes down the costs of production through wage cuts. The lack of union protection makes workers more vulnerable, and therefore decentralised bargaining is harmful to them. This discrepancy in the effects of decentralised bargaining between the north and south was recently analysed by Birindelli (2016).

The ISTAT survey confirms the existence of a strong territorial gap that penalises the south in terms of second-level bargaining system in general, and at the plant level in particular. This is extremely relevant. It can be explained by the fact that second-level bargaining was applied in a production context that evidently did not require that system. In other words, a model valid elsewhere has been applied, inappropriately, in Southern Italy.

It is therefore assumed that on the firms' part there is a gradual abandonment of this system, while on the workers' part there is instead a reduction in their bargaining power and a stagnation or reduction of their wages.

The problem then is to understand how and when to implement the decentralised bargaining system since it is not mandatory for firms, but it could be convenient given the tax breaks connected to it. In any case, it is worth mentioning a policy proposal for a second-level bargaining system, in which the productivity targets to be linked to the variable wage are established *ex-ante.* It has been called "pact for a planned productivity", and the aim is to try to stop the productivity decline that started in Italy in the mid-1990s. This proposal originated within a debate that began in 2009 with the contribution of Fadda (2009) and other economists: Antonioli and Pini (2013), Ciccarone and Messori (2013), Tridico (2014b) and Pini (2015b).

Notes

1 In this book I will not deal with the *Fornero* and *Jobs Act reforms*, respectively, issued in 2012 and in 2014. See Pini (2015a) and Forges Davanzati and Giangrande (2017b).

2   The OECD indicators of employment protection are synthetic indicators of the strictness of regulation on dismissals and the use of temporary contracts. They are compiled from 21 items covering three different aspects of employment protection regulations as they were in force on January 1st of each year.

(OECD, 2013b)

Moreover, the OECD indicators of employment protection legislation measure the procedures and costs involved in dismissing individuals or groups of workers and the procedures involved in hiring workers on fixed-term or temporary work agency contracts.

3 It appears contradictory to implement security plans in a context characterised by fiscal consolidation. This contradiction can be explained as the result of the concomitant pressure to deregulate the labour market and to reduce public spending on the welfare state (Baccaro and Tober, 2017). Indeed, according to fiscal sociology, the State must pursue two opposite aims: on one hand it has to favour capital accumulation and, on the other, it should preserve social cohesion (O'Connor, 1976).

4 The traditional criterion for measuring unemployment is no longer adequate to represent the real situation. In 2012, the CGIL's Giuseppe Di Vittorio Foundation (FDV) proposed the adoption of new parameters, elaborating another index called "Occupational Sufferance Area" (in Italian, *Area Sofferenza Occupazionale*), which considers the unemployed, discouraged people willing to work and workers that receive redundancy payment as explained by Ferrucci (2012). Later, the FDV provided another index, the "Occupational Distress Area" (in Italian, *Area Disagio Occupazionale*), which includes people who have a temporary job because they could not find a permanent one and those who have a part-time job because they could not find a full-time one (Ferrucci, 2013). Thus, the FDV tried to represent the occupational problems clearly, providing an assessment of the number of under-65-year-olds who are obliged to stay out of the labour market or those that have a different job from the one they wish for. This attempt deserves attention because it tries to outline a weighting system that was not indicated by the official statistics.

5 Wage moderation also affects the relations between firms and banks. Indeed, following Graziani's monetary circuit (Graziani, 1989), wage moderation affects credit supply and credit demand via the following channels: (i) the reduction of aggregate demand reduces the demand for most Italian firms operating on the domestic market, and (ii) this, in turn, involves a decrease of profits and reduction

of solvency (or bankruptcies), which induces banks to restrict credit supply with consequent negative effects on the path of private investment (Ramskogler, 2007). Therefore, this gives rise to deflationary pressures with the consequent further decline of both investment and consumption.

6 The increasing number of new global competitors (China, India, Brazil) also reduced the international market shares for Italian firms. In other words, two effects seem to be in operation as regards the links between wage moderation and net exports in the Italian economy: (i) insofar as the Italian production structure is mainly composed of firms operating in "mature" sectors (such as agribusiness and luxury goods, apart from the chemical, pharmaceutical and automotive sectors), exports of these goods are driven by their quality; (ii) as regards luxury goods, the so-called Veblen effect is in operation, meaning that as the unit price increases so does the volume of goods exported (Forges Davanzati, 2006).

7 Post-Keynesian scholars stress that, based on Sraffa (1960), the total factor productivity (TFP) cannot be measured. This argument is based on the conclusion that the aggregate production function cannot be constructed since, at the macroeconomic level, the measurement of capital, being a non-homogeneous good, is logically impossible. Moreover, it can be pointed out that the inclusion of the neo-Ricardian school in the Post-Keynesian theoretical framework appears disputable (Graziani, 1997).

8 An interesting emblematic case that summarises these two conceptions is the RSU, which are workers that simultaneously represent their colleagues and the trade unions. This dual representation is the compromise between the CGIL vision, which conceives the union as a representative of the workers, and the CISL concept, which sees the union as a representative of its members.

9 It seems that Article 8 of Law Decree 138 of 2011 – later converted into Law – is the response of Berlusconi's fourth government, to the letter sent to him on 5 August 2011 by Jean-Claude Trichet and Mario Draghi. This letter, signed by the then-president-in-office and the nominee of the European Central Bank (ECB) and published only on 29 September by *Corriere della Sera*, states:

> There is also a need to further reform the collective wage bargaining system allowing firm-level agreements to tailor wages and working conditions to firms' specific needs and increasing their relevance with respect to other layers of negotiations. The June 28 agreement between the main trade unions and the industrial businesses associations moves in this direction.
>
> (Trichet and Draghi, 2011)

3 The effects of the university reforms on the labour market

3.1 Introduction

Starting from the seminal papers of Gary Becker (1964), mainstream economists began to examine "human capital" whereby education is considered as an investment: it is assumed that agents spend their time and monetary resources on education in order to increase their individual chances of being hired. This particular good, composed of knowledge and skills, is considered a relevant factor both in increasing, at the microeconomic level, the individual probability of being hired and earning higher wages and, on the macroeconomic plane, in driving economic growth (OECD, 2019).

Human capital can be defined as the stock "of productive skills and knowledge acquired by individuals as income producers within a given economic system" (Praussello and Marenco, 1996). It can be assimilated through both learning by schooling and learning by doing (Arrow, 1962; Lucas, 1988). Moreover, human capital is treated as general human capital, or the stock of basic knowledge individuals obtain via schooling, and specific human capital, meaning competences obtained by doing.

Mainstream economists mainly conceive human capital accumulation as an investment and not as consumption. Indeed, in this approach, the individual agents, quite independently from the social and historical context in which they are embedded, choose whether or not to increase their own reserves of education only if the expected returns in terms of wages and status are higher than the current costs in terms of money and time (Hout, 2012; Romer, 1986).

Becker (1964) considered education and training to be the most important investments in human capital, referring to investments in which people cannot be separated from their knowledge and skills as they can be separated, for example, from their financial and physical assets. In any case, human capital can be accumulated like physical capital.

DOI: 10.4324/9781003089322-4

In mainstream labour economics, it is stressed that human capital has the following characteristics: (i) it can be conceived as a "meritorious" good; (ii) it is not transferable. Human capital is a meritorious good in the sense that there is a widespread conviction that schooling must be guaranteed to all citizens. Moreover, generally speaking, human capital is not transferable. More precisely, human capital derived from learning by schooling is transferable from one firm to another because it does not contain specific skills. In contrast, human capital derived from learning by doing is more difficult to transfer, being specific to the technology that firms use. This distinction recalls the difference between general knowledge and competences, or in other words, the difference between knowing the way something works and being able to make it work.

The view that human capital accumulation is subject to a rational choice and that it is solely an investment is subject to the following critiques:

1   Starting from the seminal book of Samuel Bowles and Herbert Gintis (1976), it is stressed that education, in a capitalist economy, is necessarily functional to capital reproduction. In other words, knowledge – and even scientific research – is *not neutral* with respect to the institutional environment where it is produced and disseminated. Even unintentionally, teaching serves the purpose of "creating" a pool of potential workers who are docile with respect to the prevailing formal, informal and moral norms which are at the basis of the capitalist power relationships. As Bowles and Gintis (1976) pointed out, a capitalist education system mainly serves the aim of "the legitimation of inequality".

2   Institutionalist scholars highlighted that the decision to invest in education cannot be a purely individual choice, for different reasons: (i) individuals are embedded in social relationships which began in their early childhood. As a result, the transmission of "soft skills" is a primary motive in deciding whether or not to improve their level of education. It is added that the transmission of "soft skills" is, in turn, a fundamental driver of increasing income inequality (Franzini and Pianta, 2016); (ii) individuals are also embedded in social relationships which significantly affect their decision to increase their level of education, regardless of their families.

3   Education is not only an investment. Indeed, it is likely to give students "utility" *per se*, such as the delight in learning how the world works. Indeed, as stressed earlier, this latter point is connected with the view that education involves a purely investment decision and that, as a result, it is subject to a rational calculus. Starting from the seminal

studies of Herbert Simon (1982), institutional economists support the idea that economic choices are made in a "reasonable" way, aiming to show that, in the case examined here, the individual decision to increase the educational level is only partially motivated by the purpose of increasing the probability of being hired.

While mainstream economists, based on Solow's model and the subsequent models of economic growth, affirm that the accumulation of human capital is the main driver of economic growth, evidence shows that this does not always occur. In particular, it does not occur in cases where human capital is not perfectly allocated in the labour market. This, in turn, may derive from a number of factors. For the sake of the argument, here I deal with the problem of overeducation, which is the most important factor (see, among others, Leuven and Oosterbeek, 2011; McGuinness, 2006). Overeducation can be defined as the problem which occurs when an individual possesses a higher education level than required for a particular job. This problem is focused mainly on the profitability of education and its consequences on job satisfaction and productivity.

Indeed, since the publication of Freeman (1976), the term "overeducation" has been contested. The subsequent debate on the economic returns on extra years of education leads to much questioning about the expansion of higher education and the labour market's capability of providing higher-skilled jobs in order to make full use of both private and public investment in education (Munsech-Capsada, 2017). In any case, the ways of measuring overeducation are varied and also controversial (Betti et al., 2011; Flisi et al., 2017; Luciano and Romanò, 2017).

In this context, the current section aims at verifying (i) if the fundamental goal of the reforms of the Italian university system (i.e. to increase the employability of graduates) has been reached (Section 3.2); (ii) if not, what are the theoretical weak points of this approach (Sections 3.3. and 3.4); (iii) if an alternative economic policy can reach better macroeconomic results (Section 3.5). It will also be shown that in the case of the reforms of the Italian education system, the same basic steps adopted for the reforms examined in the previous chapter have been applied, namely: (i) the identification of an alarmism (in this case the mismatch between labour demand and labour supply); (ii) the creation of a consensus in both academic and political circles on this alarmism and finally (iii) the implementation of an economic policy designed to tackle the problem. In the next sections, all references made to the "education system" will refer only to university reforms and never to upper secondary school reforms.

3.2 The mismatch approach and the rising unemployment of highly educated workers

The mainstream view – labelled here the educational mismatch approach – is based on Becker's seminal work (1964). It is dominant in academic and political groups, and it supports the view that education is a significant driver of economic growth and increased high-quality employment, *provided that the education system prepares workers to enter the labour market according to the competences required by firms.*

In order to achieve this result, it is argued that the education system must be organised in order to produce "employable" workers (Dal Lago, 2018). This means workers who have competences in the same field as those required by firms. Scholars who support this view argue that this intervention also has an impact on scientific research: since the aim of the University is to produce employable workers, little space should be devoted to basic research, and, more importantly, basic research (particularly in humanities and social sciences) should be characterised by a strong specialisation in the use of technical aspects, such as econometrics in political economy or cliometrics in economic history. According to this interpretation, the reforms of the education system have gone in the direction of the *de-politicisation* of scientific research, meaning that the capacity to manage a technique (e.g. a statistical technique) matters more than critical reasoning (Bellofiore, 2018a). According to this interpretation, such a path is accelerated by the criteria for the evaluation of science provided by the National Agency for the Evaluation of Scientific Research (ANVUR), which encourages conformism (Bellofiore and Vertova, 2018).

The university reforms that Italy experienced at the turn of the century were undertaken as part of the so-called "Bologna process", which aimed mainly to promote student's mobility and university course harmonisation. This view is the keystone of the "reforms" of the Italian university system in recent decades, better known by the minister's surnames than the number of the law:

1   The Zecchino–Berlinguer reform (Ministerial Decree no. 509/1999) entirely rescheduled the Italian tertiary education structure, moving to a two-tier system called "3+2", composed of two cycles: (i) a three-year degree (undergraduate) and (ii) two-year degree (master level). The aim of this reform was to boost the enrolments, to increase the number of graduates, to reduce the dropout rate and to allow students to complete their exams within the prescribed time (Aina and Casalone, 2018).

2   The Moratti reform (Law no. 53/2003) allowed the Italian universities to create postgraduate programmes regardless of the previous

undergraduate course done and to link them to the local firms' demands. The aim of this reform was to connect tertiary education to the labour market, supporting the needs of the local production structure.

3 The Mussi reform (Ministerial Decree no. 544/2007) rescheduled the courses and limited the exam credit bonus from extra-academic activity.
4 The Gelmini Reform (Law no. 240/2010) cut public funding to Italian universities, enhanced the role of ANVUR, changed university professors' recruitment and reshaped the courses.

It should be stressed that the public debate involving Parliament, political parties, the Conference of Italian University Rectors (CRUI) and the National University Council (CUN) has been replaced by the decisions made by some experts. Normally, these experts have been designated by the MIUR – and later by ANVUR – in order to make a silent reform of the university system. Despite the political differences between the coalitions in power, all the Italian Governments from 1999 to 2010 reformed the university system in order to adapt its educational mission to the needs of the labour market, namely to transform Italian universities into agencies able to produce employable workers.

Moreover, all these reforms have been implemented without any clear debate. Indeed, in the public debate, Italian universities have been described by the mainstream media as places of corruption (Stella and Rizzo, 2010) and nepotism (Grilli and Allesina, 2017), using the rhetoric of "waste" of public money (Forges Davanzati and Paulì, 2015). Consequently, a denigration campaign against the university system was conducted without any possibility of serious debate as would be required for an issue that is crucial for the whole country. In short, a crusade was launched in favour of meritocracy[1] and against public funding of disadvantaged areas. As a result, there is a widespread view, supported by the mainstream economic theory and with significant consequences in terms of economic policy that:

1 since there are too many universities and most of them are inefficient, public funds should be allocated only to some universities, those with higher performance as measured by ANVUR (Giavazzi, 2013);
2 given that university professors do not work hard, produce inferior research and are not rewarded on their merits, they should be hired and assessed in a different way from the system used in the past (Artoni, 2007; Beltratti, 2007; Garegnani, 2007; Lippi and Peracchi, 2007);
3 considering that the students would like to study closer to their hometown, and that they do not complete their exams within the set time period, they should be encouraged to move towards better universities (Cersosimo et al., 2016);

4   the lack of graduate employability, imputed to the Italian university's tendency to provide generic knowledge (the so-called Humboldtian model), creates the urgent need to modify the degree courses and make them more relevant to the local labour market.

In this context, the national university budget (in Italian *Fondo Finanziamento Ordinario* or FFO) has been cut by around 20% (Viesti, 2018) mainly through:

1   the block on staff turnover (Vertova, 2018), which means fewer and fewer professors, the increase in professors' average age with no chance for young academics to be tenured after years and years of precarious working conditions;
2   the decrease of national financing and regional funds for scholarships, housing and facilities, which means reduced opportunities for students.

These interventions were motivated by a double aim: (i) to reduce public spending (in a fiscal consolidation regime) and (ii) to increase the number of graduates. Leaving aside the first aim, I will try to verify whether the second goal has been reached in the period under consideration.

From 2008, Italian universities reacted to the funding cuts by increasing their fees (UDU, 2018). This caused:

1   a drop in enrolments, particularly for students from lower-income families, from the *Mezzogiorno*, and from technical and professional secondary schools;
2   fewer students and, therefore, fewer graduates in Italy (Viesti, 2016);
3   the need to look for private financing, which depends on the economic and entrepreneurial context in which each university is embedded.

In fact, evidence shows that there is a gap between the expected outcomes and the outcomes achieved. According to data elaborated by Nuvolari and Vasta (2015), in 1975, the public and private spending on R&D in Italy was 0.8% of GDP, while in 1990 it was 1.3%. The R&D average in OECD countries in the same years was 1.3% and 1.6%, respectively. In those years (1975–1990), there was a convergence trend of R&D towards the other industrialised countries. Italy's convergence trajectory on R&D spending declined in 1995, falling to 1% of GDP while the OECD average rose further.

This path has stopped since the Great Recession (2007–2008), when the fourth Berlusconi government reacted by cutting funds for research. In the same period, the then-Economy and Finance Minister, Giulio Tremonti, is alleged to have said that "you cannot eat culture" (Dubini, 2019). In 2010, Italy reduced the quality and size of universities (Fondazione Res, 2016) and fell to the bottom of the ranking among industrialised countries, overtaken also by Spain (Felice, 2015).

By looking at the data provided by ISTAT, it is possible to understand how the labour market changed from 1977 to 2018. Indeed, the employment data reveals important details on the workers' education levels:

1   in 1987, the number of workers with lower secondary education (7.5 million) overtook the workers with no education or primary education (7 million);
2   in 1991, the workers with upper secondary education (5.8 million) overtook the workers with no education or primary education (5.6 million);
3   in 1998, the workers with upper secondary education (7.9 million) overtook the workers with lower secondary education (almost 7.8 million);
4   in 2001 the workers with tertiary education (2.7 million) overtook the workers with no education or with primary education (2.4 million).

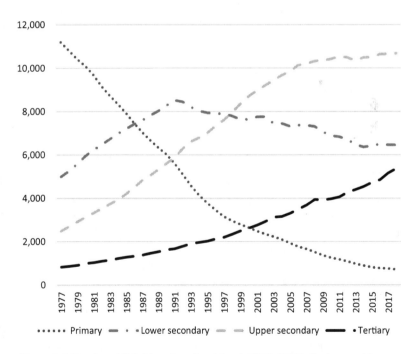

Figure 3.1 Employed (15+) by educational level (1977–2018) (in thousands)
Source: My elaboration on ISTAT data

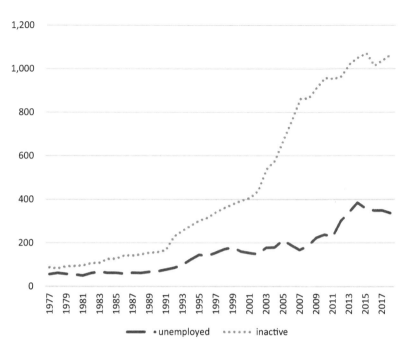

Figure 3.2 Unemployed (15+) and inactive (15–64) with tertiary education (1977–2018) (in thousands)

Source: My elaboration on ISTAT data

Despite the percentage of workers with tertiary education in the Italian labour market rising from 4.2% in 1977 to 23.1% in 2018, the higher-educated workers are still fewer in number than those with lower and upper secondary-level education. Moreover, in 2009, 40.3% of those with tertiary education were overeducated for the job they were doing (Curtarelli and Gualtieri, 2011).

The data about unemployment and inactivity from 1977 to 2018 show that people with tertiary education were generally less affected by both phenomena. It is worth highlighting that among the unemployed (15+) and the inactive (15–64) with tertiary education, the largest proportion has always been the latter. In any case, the divergence trend has become stronger since the 1990s.

Moreover, the number of workers with tertiary education in part-time employment is growing. ISTAT finds that they would be willing to increase their working hours, and, based on their response, ISTAT itself defines them as "involuntary part-time workers".

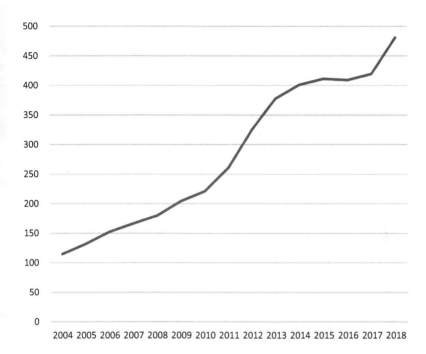

Figure 3.3 Employed workers (15+) with tertiary education and an involuntary part-time job (2004–2018) (in thousands)

Source: My elaboration on ISTAT data

According to the ISTAT (2018), in five years, Italy has lost over 156,000 people with medium and high education levels. In 2017, 52.6% of Italian citizens who moved abroad had upper secondary and tertiary qualifications: there were around 33,000 school graduates and 28,000 university graduates. Compared to 2016, the number of school graduates who emigrated was stable while the university graduates slightly increased (+3.9%). However, the increase is much more marked if we consider a wider time span. Indeed, compared to 2013, the number of school graduates emigrating increased by 32.9% and university graduates by 41.8%. ISTAT (2018) points out that the main reason driving young Italians to leave Italy is the negative trend of the Italian labour market, which pushes the most educated and qualified young people to move towards those countries where there are better job and career opportunities and higher wages.

However, in recent decades, profound changes have occurred in the university sector, which have altered its size and quality. Indeed, the Italian university system experienced a historical transition from an elite one to a

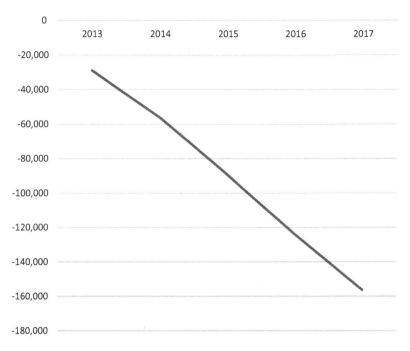

Figure 3.4 People with upper secondary and tertiary education emigrating (2013–2017) (cumulative data)

Source: My elaboration on ISTAT data

mass one in 1969 (Ginsborg, 2006). For the first time in Italian history, the number of university students is now falling. For over a decade, there has been a systematic decline in enrolments.

All the main indicators of the last 15 years confirm the trend of the Italian university system decline: number of enrolments, dropout rate, graduates, professors, employees and funding. Certainly, the 2007–2008 global financial crisis and the funding cuts from MIUR to universities have accentuated the difficulties of lower-income families, who can no longer bear the cost of tertiary education for their children due to the increase in university tuition fees. Fees rose by 57.5% between 2004/05 and 2013/14 (OECD, 2013a), with a heavier burden in the less developed Italian regions (UDU, 2018). In its entirety, all these variables show the huge disinvestment that Italy has carried out in contrast with the most advanced and emerging countries. Furthermore, in Italy, the spending cuts in the university sector were greater than in other public sectors. In short, Italy is disinvesting in its tertiary education system and is doing so especially in the weakest regions of the country, precisely in those areas where a university can play an important role in economic and social development (Agasisti et al., 2019).

Private funding for the Italian university system has grown, but the capacity to raise this kind of resources does not depend on the ability of the universities to attract extra funds but on the entrepreneurial context of their territories.

Moreover, a system of differentiation is emerging among Italian universities, with a range of structural features in terms of funding, professors, students and internationalisation. In this system – which is reasonably similar to the USA's teaching universities and research universities – the former will prepare the undergraduate students, who will then be selected by the latter for postgraduate and advanced training (Forges Davanzati, 2016). The research universities would be located presumably in the north of Italy (ROARS, 2019), in particular in the 200 km triangle between Milan–Bologna–Venice (Viesti, 2016).

The university system reforms implemented in Italy in recent decades have been essentially based on the postulate of the university as an agent with the task of introducing "employable" people into the labour market, in a short-term functionalist perspective. In essence, the reference point has become the growth of skills and not of knowledge.

In conclusion, Italian education policies have been implemented exclusively as a potential solution for economic problems such as the reduction of public spending in order to generate primary surpluses, or the proposals for a recovery of public spending for the university sector aiming to increase exports. The first objective has partially failed not only because the austerity measures adopted since 2010 have generated savings in the public sector but also because the growth of the public debt/GDP ratio has been due to the drop in GDP. The second objective is related more with the Italian production structure, which is only partially oriented towards exports.

3.3 An alternative approach

The theoretical approach discussed in this section, which can be inserted into the Post-Keynesian framework, is founded on the idea that education *may* drive economic growth only insofar as firms express a labour demand which is consistent with the level and the quality of the human capital formed in upper secondary schools and in universities. In other words, Post-Keynesian scholars stress that increasing human capital *per se* may not produce positive macroeconomic outcomes, unless the economic production structure is in a position to hire highly educated people. Moreover, they stress that employment of young workers does not depend entirely on the education system and its link with private firms, but basically depends on whether or not there is a lack of aggregate demand. It is argued that the increasing unemployment and inactivity of highly educated people is basically due to the Italian production structure and its firms' specialisation, as well as the size of the Italian public sector and its current disinclination to hire high-skilled workers.

On the theoretical plane, it is argued that as aggregate demand varies so does labour productivity, through variations of investment in human capital. This is an augmented version of the Kaldor–Verdoorn Law, which seems to fit the Italian case in the period under consideration. Evidence shows that in recent decades labour demand for high-skilled workers has fallen dramatically. At the same time, labour supply of high-skilled workers has fallen too, as a result of the lower number of graduates.

A vicious circle seems to be in place, involving the changes in labour demand and its effect on the labour supply. In other words, due to the operation of the learning effect, as labour demand for high-educated/high-skilled workers falls, so does the probability of being hired. Arguably, this modifies workers' expectations on the returns on their investment in education, which, in turn, pushes them not to increase it. This is a case of interaction between labour demand and labour supply, in which the overall result should be:

1   a decline of labour productivity, insofar as the aggregate stock of human capital is lower than it would be in the event of high labour demand for high-skilled workers;
2   a decline of domestic demand imputed to low consumption, insofar as low-skilled workers receive, as a norm, a lower wage than high-skilled workers (OECD, 2019).

In this theoretical framework, an initial reduction of both public and private spending on R&D, which negatively affects domestic demand, generates a subsequent reduction of the proportion of high-skilled workers in the total labour force. Hence, there is a further decline of both domestic demand and the rate of growth of labour productivity. This is a typical case of a vicious CCC *à la Myrdal* (1957), which is in line with the Kaldorian theoretical framework (Kaldor, 1966) at the basis of the analysis provided here.

ISTAT certifies that, in 2012, 95.2% of the 4.4 million Italian firms employed from 1–9 employees, representing 46.7% of the total 16.7 million workers in Italy in that year. About 77.3% of the Italian firms were in the sector comprising commerce, transport, hotels and other services (ISTAT, 2014), and they employed 65.9% of the total workforce. In contrast, the firms in the industrial sector – considered in the strict sense and,

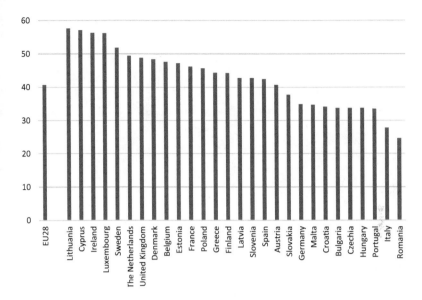

Figure 3.5 Population aged 30–34 with tertiary educational attainment (ISCED 5–8) (2018)

Source: My elaboration on EUROSTAT data (2018)

therefore, without the building sector – constituted only 9.9% of the total and employed 24.8% of the workforce.

Moreover, Italy is second-to-last in the EU rankings for the percentage of young people between 30 and 34 years with a tertiary education level compared to the total population, with 27.8% as opposed to 40.7% in the EU-28.

This decline can be partially explained by the Italian demographic decline (ISTAT, 2019), but there are also many other factors that determine the decision to continue tertiary studies: the social, cultural and economic conditions of the families of origin, how the upper secondary school institutions work and the reason for university dropouts (Aina and Casalone, 2018). Concerns are also growing about an economic system that does not value higher education and about the sense of the investment in view of the worsening of employment conditions and graduates' wages (Banca d'Italia, 2018).

Most economists recognise that economic activities in the future will increasingly be based on innovation and a highly qualified workforce. Workers will need more and more knowledge and skills to carry out different, non-repetitive and creative tasks (Brynjolfsson and McAfee, 2014).

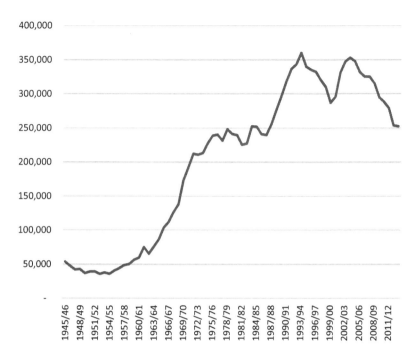

Figure 3.6 New entrants in university (1945/46–2013/14)

Source: My elaboration on ISTAT data

Therefore, the industrialised countries' competitiveness will depend on a production structure based on highly labour-intensive and highly educated and skilled workers. Italy's situation shows that having graduates does not in itself guarantee that the economic system is competitive (Viesti, 2018). Indeed, if industrial policies are not linked with research and innovation, the production system will not be able to absorb new graduates and use them optimally.[2]

The Italian paradox is having few graduates in an economy that should be based on knowledge and, at the same time, leaving them underutilised or, even worse, letting them emigrate abroad. The overeducation phenomenon cripples investment in tertiary education while undereducation should call attention to the low education level that prevents competition with more advanced countries.

Evidence shows that most Italian firms compete via wage moderation (see Chapter 2) and confirms that the Italian private sector does not produce innovations and, at the best, tends to import them (Lucarelli and Romano, 2015). Some critical scholars deem that the public investment in tertiary

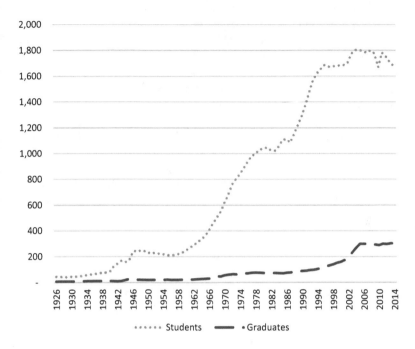

Figure 3.7 University students and graduates (1926–2014) (in thousands)
Source: My elaboration on ISTAT data

education and research is crucial (Viesti, 2018), and that the role of the university system is strategic for economic and social development because the acquisition of human capital is fundamental for the production of innovative quality goods and services. However, this is quite a new consensus which has emerged in more recent years and does not seem to be dominant in political circles. These researchers add that the Italian university system needs to be financed as a whole, without distinctions between universities located in the most developed or less developed areas of Italy (Fondazione Res, 2016). This view strongly opposes the mainstream narrative that argues – as emphasised earlier – that the Italian university system is a locus of corruption and that it should be funded on a selective basis, on the grounds of performance in terms of number of graduates who have completed their exams within the prescribed time and the quality of scientific research.

The view that Italy needs to return to a path of economic growth via innovation is reinforced by the acceleration of technological advancement on a global scale – named the "fourth industrial revolution", which involves a radical revision of education systems, as requested by the most up-to-date business organisations in order to identify the ongoing techno-logical changes and potentially to produce them.

This policy in Italy is known as *Industria 4.0*, and it is based on the edu-cation system with a short-term vision of the role that widespread education can play on economic growth. This view overlooks the fact that in an econ-omy with rapid technological advancement the skills acquired today tend to become obsolete quickly, and that what should be done is to strengthen critical learning skills.

The reference to the function of research at the service of competitive-ness – which is the basis of the recent reforms of the Italian university sys-tem – risks being misleading.

First of all, scientific research produces long-term results and, as is well known, the outcome cannot be absolutely certain. Not surprisingly, the main innovations in the history of twentieth-century capitalism were made possi-ble through a prior public investment in R&D, due to the fact that inventions can become useful innovations for private firms only in some conditions, as in so-called "patient capital" (Mazzucato, 2014).

This explains why private firms find it more convenient to use inven-tions that have already been perfected using public funding, if there are the conditions to transform innovations into profits. This applies even more to basic research (e.g. research in mathematics or in the humanities), where the results are more uncertain and long-term than in applied research (e.g. engineering sectors).

The issue raised by Mazzucato (2014) – that is, the historically veri-fied need for a prior public production of innovations in order to generate innovations in the private sector – gives rise to an objection concerning the coherence between innovative processes and satisfaction of social needs (Pennacchi, 2018). The question can be tackled in the following terms. When the knowledge produced by the public actor is taken over by the private sector, the political inclination towards innovations to apply to the social context is lost, and there is a risk that the innovations will be used solely to create false needs.

The interaction between knowledge reproduction and capitalist reproduc-tion is currently, and particularly in Italy, of a short-term kind.

The particular condition of the current phase is the set of massive global processes of financialisation. In contexts where the financialisation of the economy does not have a structural character, as in Italy, firms react in every possible way to the need for production and sale of goods/services at ever smaller time intervals. Therefore, there are clear elements of intrinsic contradiction in the mechanism. Firms are asking the education system to produce technical knowledge at the same pace as the production and sale of goods/services, which proceed faster and faster.

Hence, it is evident that in the current context, characterised by rapid technological advancement and innovative processes, it will not be necessary for the education system to provide quick "know how", but the "know how to learn", since the skills acquired today will become obsolete in a short time.

It is therefore clear that there is an inconsistency between the objectives set and the path to reach them. To all this, it must be added that an under-funded education system (hence, with increasing university tuition fees) accentuates the relational links of the labour market (Franzini and Pianta, 2016) and blocks social mobility (CENSIS, 2019).

Generally speaking, it can be argued that education policies follow capitalist cycles, which means that in the technological advancement stage, the spending on education tends to grow and tends to be based on technical skills.

There is no doubt that the fourth industrial revolution will have significant effects, which are currently largely unpredictable, on the reconfiguration of the labour market.[3]

It can be observed that a technical advancement, at least in the sectors and economies in which it is implemented, tends to be deflationary as it increases labour productivity and, above all, tends to be associated with a wage decrease (at least for low-skilled workers). In a context that is already characterised by deflationary dynamics, the fourth industrial revolution, in the absence of corrective public interventions, could accentuate this spiral.

The conjecture that the current technological revolution will make the labour market increasingly dualistic – with uncertain effects on the growth of the unemployment rate due to technical advancement (Gallino, 1998)– appears reasonable. It is therefore considered likely that there will be a polarisation between highly paid workers with very specific skills and a mass of unskilled workers in the services sector. There is also likely to be an increase of labour demand in the caregiving sector due to the aging of the population (ISTAT, 2019).[4]

Moreover, technical advancement is an essential tool to allow the firms that adopt it to increase the capital turnover rate, winning market shares and making profits in the shortest possible time between production and sale.[5] This is a case where competition among firms is time-based, that is the individual firm is forced by the competitive pressure to produce and sell before its competitors. Based on the aforementioned hypothesis – that is the interaction between labour demand and labour supply – one can expect that if firms increase their capital turnover, this would involve an increase in innovation, a further increase in the demand for high-skilled labour and, due to the improvement of workers' expectations on their probability of being hired, an increase in aggregate investment in education.

Finally, it is interesting to observe the discrepancy between public education policies and university research, along with the growing disaffection shown by some universities, the business world and, in reflection, by some politicians regarding the "rigidity" of the degree courses introduced by the latest reforms. This fracture is shown by the call for (i) a greater interdisciplinarity; (ii) lower investment in skills and greater investment in knowledge and critical thinking in order to internalise mental habits functional to learning.

In this scenario, there is likely to be an accentuation of polarisation effects of education systems – effects already underway – aimed at: (i) cranking out high-skilled workers in the areas of the country with a greater concentration of innovative firms and (ii) supplying low-skilled workers in peripheral regions.

In essence, while CCC schemes envisage that firms establish their production in areas where excellent pre-existing research centres are located (in addition to agglomeration effects deriving from the existence of networks and low transport costs, with consequent economies of scale), it seems, on the other hand, that the technological changes underway favour a different, opposing tendency: research centres are considered "excellent" (through greater public and private financing) in the areas where there is a pre-existing business concentration.

3.4 The PhD and its impact on the labour market

In this section, I will show how the university reforms have had a negative impact on the productivity and health of non-tenured scholars.

Everything started when the Spanish newspaper *El País* recently published an article written by Pablo Barrecheguren (2018) dealing with the psychological problems that afflict PhD students. The article, which cites two scientific research studies published in *Research Policy* and in *Nature Biotechnology*, has opened a debate in Italy by bringing to the general public's attention the academic problem of young researchers' emotional health.

The first paper (Levecque et al., 2017), drafted by the University of Ghent (Belgium), takes a sample of 3,659 PhD students from Flemish universities who follow a doctorate course similar to those that are attended in the rest of Europe and in the United States of America. The study quantifies the frequency with which the doctoral students state they have experienced in the last few weeks one of the parameters considered signs of stress (unhappiness, under pressure, loss of self-esteem, insomnia, depression). The results of this study show interesting percentages: 41% feel under pressure; 30% are depressed or unhappy; 28% have lost sleep; 25% have loss of self-esteem; 16% feel useless. The study concludes that the development of these symptoms is independent of the PhD research field and that PhD students show more frequent symptoms of deterioration in mental health compared to other groups of workers with high levels of education and training. The second study (Evans et al., 2018), conducted by researchers affiliated to different American faculties and departments reports that 39% of PhD students present a moderate or serious depression profile as compared to 6% of the rest of the population. This study shows that PhD students are six times more at risk of developing anxiety or depression than the rest of the population. A particularly widespread condition is the so-called "impostor syndrome", which is characterised by the idea of not deserving the position and the success obtained. This expression was coined by Clance and Imes (1978) in the context of research on successful women, and it can be applied very well also to the academic context. Indeed, it is thought to push those who suffer from this psychological distress to further efforts – which include giving up sleep and social life – to fill the alleged gaps in knowledge and skills (Vadacchino and Nardi, 2019).

Taking into account the fact that precarious work involves the risk of getting depressed and that this is not only a problem for workers – who lose their emotional well-being – but also for firms, which lose productivity (Moscone et al., 2016), it is important to start questioning emotional health issues in academia.

It is fundamental to analyse the widespread precariousness in Italian academia recorded by the data elaborated by the CGIL's Knowledge Workers' Union Federation (FLC-CGIL) (Grüning and Russo, 2018) and by the Association of PhD students and young researchers in Italy (ADI, 2019). The focus should be the emotions caused in PhD students, post-doctoral students and non-tenured researchers (hereinafter referred to as young academics). Indeed, all these young academics are part of the strategic sector called "research", in which innovations are generated not only for the private sector but also for the whole society and which, in turn, brings economic growth (Mazzucato, 2014).

Both the papers mentioned earlier show us that in Italy there is the lack of an overall study highlighting all that is discussed privately and under-discussed in those few moments when young academics exchange views on their own professional life with other colleagues. The Italian situation presents similarities with the results described in the studies conducted by Levecque et al. (2017) and by Evans et al. (2018) but presents some particularly interesting differences linked to an economic context based on wage moderation and fiscal consolidation underway since the 1990s.

The research studies published by SVIMEZ (2019) and by Fondazione Res (2016) show that the underfunding of the national public university system, which has been underway for over a decade, has now reached a level that prefigures the downsizing, or closure, of universities in the South of Italy. This concern is confirmed by the recent news regarding the establishment of a Big League of Italian Universities decided by ANVUR (ROARS, 2019).

As shown earlier, the underfunding of Italian universities has three effects: (i) reduction of enrolments and subsequent increase in university tuition fees, placing a greater burden on low- and middle-income families, transforming Italian universities into places increasingly frequented by students from higher income families; (ii) the kind of labour demand expressed by Italian firms is supported by the deskilling of the workforce as the Italian production structure – except very rare exceptions – does not need highly skilled workers; (iii) the pervasiveness of external funding to the university system (e.g. by firms, regional, national and European calls for tenders) not only tends to exclude important disciplinary sectors but also means that the subject matter of the research commissioned may be far-removed from the research interests of young academics.

The macroeconomic context and the long period of precarious work experienced and foreseen supposedly acts as a disciplinary mechanism for young academics like the worker discipline device described by Shapiro and Stiglitz (1984) in relation to unemployment. In this case, I am talking about young academics whose job renewal does not depend on their academic commitment and outcomes but on the availability of funds – which are distributed in an increasingly unequal manner among the universities – and also on the importance of their own superiors in the relevant disciplinary sectors.

The ADI has calculated that 90.5% of researchers in Italian universities will lose their positions in the university system in the coming years (ADI, 2019). The ever lower hopes for young academics to obtain standard employment combined with the economic instability are all factors that make the first period of an academic career a source of discomfort and malaise (Coin, 2019). Messages of profound emotional distress are launched daily, but most of them remain unheard. In recent years, several young Italian academics have reported poor working conditions and rigged selection examinations, with some of them even resorting to an irreversible act such as suicide.

The development of these negative emotions can be found:

1   in the daily pressure on young academics to respond to assessments based on the parameters and criteria established by the MIUR and ANVUR;
2   in the ways in which tenured professors as supervisors guide and control the working and relaxation time of their students and, finally, the relationship they develop with their supervisees.

Massimo Piermattei, a former researcher in the history of European integration, describes this situation very well. In July 2017, he decided to continue his professional life outside the university sector. To do so, he wrote a farewell letter that triggered a brief debate on the health of researchers and the difficulties encountered by them during their academic career in Italy (Piermattei, 2017). Even the Italian movie, with the trilogy *I Can Quit Whenever I Want*, directed by Sydney Sibilia, has ironically shown the dramatic level of academic precariousness that forces a group of promising young researchers to pursue a criminal career in order to survive.

It is clear that this is a systemic phenomenon and is not confined to sporadic personal episodes. It is necessary to make a profound examination of the specific links between working conditions and mental health in Italian universities in order to take seriously the matter of the emotional well-being of their youngest employees.

Underemployment, unemployment and intellectual emigration of highly educated and skilled people are causes that can be attributed to the inability of the current Italian production structure to absorb them as workers. One can add that competition among students forces the individual student to invest more in education. As the number of educated people increases (along with labour supply) and/or labour demand for high-skilled workers falls, there is less and less probability of being hired at the expected status level in the labour market. This leads to a situation where the quality of the workforce declines, involving a decrease of human capital and the consequent lowering of labour productivity, both in the short and in the long run.

The lack of data on the scientific research path of young scholars in Italy prevents from providing a figure to link the deterioration of human capital with their productivity. In any case, it is reasonable to conclude that the continuous reduction of public spending on academic and scientific research, which aims to reduce the available vacancies and to increase the competition, produces the opposite effect, lowering the morale of young academics and, therefore, their productivity. This particular effect will be the object of a specific inquiry for future research.

3.5 The State as innovator of first resort: a policy proposal

In this section, I will discuss a recent policy proposal – that is the State as innovator of first resort – designed to counteract overeducation and, at the same time, to promote labour productivity growth via human capital growth (Bellofiore and Vertova, 2014; Colacchio and Forges Davanzati, 2019b).

On the basis of the previous analysis, two basic conclusions are in order:

1   the Italian private sector does not spontaneously produce innovation and, as a result, does not express a demand for high-skilled workers;
2   although the number of graduates tends to fall, the Italian labour market is characterised by high levels of young high-skilled unemployed workers.

In this scenario, some economists propose a massive State intervention to counteract the problem, in the form of the so-called State as innovator of first resort (Bellofiore and Vertova, 2014; Colacchio and Forges Davanzati, 2019b).

The basic idea – which is Kaldorian in essence – is that, assuming that economic growth is driven by the interaction between the increase in aggregate demand and the increase in labour productivity, higher public spending on R&D activities in the public sector is expected to generate positive macroeconomic outcomes.

The starting point of this idea – which transfers into an economic policy proposal – is that there are a number of channels which link the increase in the size of the public sector and the path of labour productivity: for instance, infrastructures and welfare services. Post-Keynesian scholars scrutinised this issue, moving within a theoretical framework where increasing public spending has positive effects on the path of labour productivity. An extension of this view has been proposed based on the operation of the so-called Kaldor–Verdoorn Law (Colacchio and Forges Davanzati, 2017; Forges Davanzati et al., 2017; Lampa and Perri, 2014). Less attention has been devoted to the possibility that expansionary fiscal policies are used to generate innovations by means of increasing gross domestic expenditure on R&D. This would lead to the idea that the role of the State is not only that of employer of last resort (Caffè, 1990; Minsky, 2014), but also of innovator of first resort.

This could particularly apply in economies where the private sector is unable to generate innovations spontaneously. The idea that the State can produce innovations is not new, and it has been proposed in different ways. First, as emphasised by Mazzucato (2014), the State provides a stock of basic knowledge which is at the basis of innovations in the private sector. Second, it has been argued that the State can directly produce innovations – so-called social-driven innovation – for the purpose of satisfying social needs, which the private sector has no interest in fulfilling (Vertova, 2014).

As shown earlier, in most cases, Italian private firms mainly demand low-skilled workers, possibly because of their small sizes and low propensity to innovate. Therefore, high-skilled workers make up a considerable part of the unemployed. In this respect, Italy is a significant case study, on two grounds: (i) the size of the Italian public sector has been dramatically reduced in the last few decades (Bianco et al., 2018; Fondazione Di Vittorio and Funzione Pubblica CGIL, 2018) through strong privatisation (Florio, 2014), combined with a massive reduction of gross domestic expenditure on R&D; (ii) the unemployment rate of young and high-skilled workers has massively increased.

The size of the public sector affects the performance of the private sector and, particularly, the path of labour productivity (Forges Davanzati and Giangrande, 2019b). It is well-known that labour productivity in Italy is lower than most OECD and European countries and that it has been continuously declining since the early 1990s. Post-Keynesian scholars support the view that the so-called Italian economic decline is to be imputed to the effects of the continuous decline of net public spending on productivity growth, according to the Kaldor–Verdoorn effect (Lampa and Perri, 2014).

Importantly, the continuous decline of productivity growth – starting from the beginning of the 1990s – can be largely explained by the continuous reduction of both private and public investment, particularly in R&D (Bugamelli et al., 2012).

The main possible criticism of this view lies in the prevailing belief, in Italian academic and political circles, that the Italian public sector is inefficient. As a result, there is the demand for a policy designed to encourage a managerial approach. The increased efficiency of the public sector is conceived as a necessary condition if private firms are to invest (Paolazzi, 2014). A similar argument is applied to universities: it is argued that they are unable to provide students with competences consistent with the demands of the private sector. Accordingly, the Italian unemployment is assumed to depend on the mismatch between labour supply and labour demand.

A policy of expansion of the public sector, particularly for R&D activities, would produce significant macroeconomic outcomes:

1   It would directly involve more *high-skilled* workers hired by the State in order to produce innovations. This would lead to an increase in the rate of growth of labour productivity, giving rise to a potential virtuous circle between increasing aggregate demand and increasing productivity.
2   It would mainly involve young workers, which, as a norm, are more productive than older workers. This effect would (at least partially) compensate the average wage of older workers employed in the Italian public sector. Arguably, the sector's inefficiency depends more on this than on the lack of managerial attitudes.

3   It would have a positive impact on domestic aggregate demand, not only because of the increased money wage bill but also because of the higher propensity to consume on the part of young workers.

4   This policy proposal also aimed at expanding the creation of good jobs, counteracting the increasing propensity of private firms to use underpaid workers (often in a condition of intellectual underemployment).

5   Above all, it would be able to tackle a paradox: a *reserve army* formed also by young high-skilled workers, unemployed or underemployed, ready to emigrate and prepared to work in R&D activities cannot get jobs in the public sector even though the few workers hired by the Italian public sector are older.

Consider also that the programme of the State as the innovator of first resort should not provoke a strong reaction from the capitalist class, insofar as increased productivity would also benefit the private sector, which could take advantage of the pool of inventions. This is especially in view of the fact that most Italian firms import high value-added capital goods. Accordingly, at least in the Italian case, this programme should not necessarily compromise private firms' competitiveness and could reduce the dependence of the Italian economy on innovation produced abroad.

Some scholars emphasise that since increased employment in the public sector increases aggregate demand, it also stimulates an increase in employment in the private sector (Wray, 2019). A similar mechanism may be in operation as regards the channel of transmission of innovations from the public to the private sector. An increase in aggregate demand resulting from the increase in employment in the public sector stimulates innovations in the private sector, not only because of the operation of the Kaldor–Verdoorn Law, but also because as the employment rate increases, it becomes more difficult for private firms to gain competitiveness via wage moderation. A Kaldorian accelerator effect is in operation here (Kaldor, 1981): as public investment increases, so does private investment.

This argument leads to conclude that:

1   an increase in net public spending on R&D activities, in some periods and/or in some countries, would produce positive effects on economic growth in a short-run perspective, via the expansion of domestic demand;

2   if the dynamics of labour productivity is taken into consideration and linked to the direction of economic policy, the result is that the performance of the economy is endogenously generated by a dynamic interaction between rising aggregate demand and growing labour productivity (Bellofiore, 2019).

In conclusion, a note of caution is in order, as stressed, among others, by Kriesler and Halevi (2001) in a Kaleckian theoretical framework. Otherwise, provided that Italy could achieve the political conditions to implement a policy of innovation driven by the public sector, this would radically change the direction of economic policy on two grounds. First, private firms would be forced to compete via innovation, so that wage moderation would no longer be on the political agenda. Second, a policy of financing of public R&D would be necessary, leading to the conclusion that Italian economic growth would no longer be profit-driven (and hence based on wage moderation) but driven by public investment and the consequent effects on private investment.

Notes

1 For a critique of the "meritocracy" ideology (Young, 1958), see Borrelli (2015).
2 The deep territorial gap between the Italian regions (SVIMEZ, 2019) acts as a brake on the overall development of the whole of Italy because, as is well known, the competitiveness of a country always comes from the competitiveness of all its territories. Indeed, Italy's development, first of all, requires the recovery of its less developed regions, mainly located in the *Mezzogiorno*. In a context like this, the presence of a quality university becomes a crucial factor for local economic development (Pasimeni, 2016), for political participation and for cultural and social life. It should be sufficient to recall that in small- and medium-sized Italian cities, the university acts as an important component of the local economy, as employer and also as buyer of local goods and services (Viesti, 2016).
3 Schematically, there are two opposing positions on this issue, reflecting long-standing attitudes (hostility or fervent support) for technical advances. The first holds that new technologies will generate technological unemployment only in the short term. In the long run, the unemployed will be spontaneously reabsorbed into other sectors, especially in the allied industries that will arise following the technical advance. The second position is based on the belief that technological unemployment will, in a sense, become a structural feature, which will make it necessary to provide the unemployed with welfare payments, also to create markets for the new products.
4 It should be remembered that the number of employees has steadily increased, despite the fact that the 1980–2015 period saw the unfolding of the most important technological revolution that capitalism has ever experienced.
5 Therefore, the real risk for Italy is not so much a massive unemployment boom but a further gap in comparison with the core countries of capitalist development. This is also due to the fact that the current processes of concentration take place outside national borders, laying the foundations for a reproduction, within the OECD area, of the unequal exchange mechanisms traditionally found in underdeveloped countries (by which the poorer areas export goods at lower prices than the goods imported from the rich areas).

Conclusions

This book is a contribution to the heated debate on Italian economic stagnation triggered by Luciano Gallino's work (2003), which opened the way to an interesting dispute. The broad discussion did not achieve any consensus, neither on the variables that indicated the Italian economic decline nor on the causes that generated it.

There was tension between scholars that attributed the Italian decline to single causes such as the adoption of the euro, the institutional weakness of Italy, the high public debt and the rigidity of the labour market. In contrast to the mainstream views, I deem that the decline is not determined only by one cause but involves all the components of the aggregate demand, which are affected by many factors such as production structure, industrial relations, demographic trends, labour policies, education policies and that the main indicator of the decline is the reduction, or stagnation, of the growth rate of labour productivity.

This book dealt with the stagnation of the Italian economy, in a theoretical framework which combines Kaleckian and Kaldorian elements. From Kalecki, I drew the idea that economic policy has a class nature, depending on the relative bargaining powers of firms and workers in the labour market. From Kaldor, I took the idea that the path of labour productivity is dependent on output growth, in accordance with the so-called Kaldor–Verdoorn Law, and that the increase in aggregate demand is the main driver of economic growth both in the short and long run.

The main argument I have put forward is the following. Starting from the beginning of the 1990s, Italy experienced a constant reduction of both private and public investment, which, combined with increasing labour precariousness and wage moderation, contributed to the decline of both labour productivity and economic growth.

The lack of industrial policies amplified the problem of the poor macroeconomic performance, since Italian firms – mainly small-sized and non-innovating – were incapable of staying competitive on the global

DOI: 10.4324/9781003089322-5

scene. Net exports did not compensate for the decline of public spending, private investment and consumption. For the sake of the argument, Italy is an interesting case-study, as it was involved in the global process of intensifying the neoliberal agenda in relatively recent times, but at a faster rate than other OECD countries. This particularly applies to labour flexibilisation and the "reforms" of the education systems, mainly in the university sector.

I showed that policies aiming at generating wage moderation were implemented as a consequence of the creation of economic alarmism, based on Federico Caffè's arguments (1972), which aimed to distort the economic situation, to inflate the negative aspects and to fabricate the impression of a continuous emergency about the economic conditions with excessive emphasis on a real problem which is presented as the most important problem to solve, in which everything should be sacrificed in favour of public debt reduction, cuts in public spending and wage moderation.

These alarmisms were created in the political circles, legitimated in the academia and propagated by the media as the major economic problem that must be solved. In any case, even if they may reflect real problems – such as inflation, rigidity, mismatch – they were considered the necessary premise in order to implement economic policies which went in the direction of reforming the labour market and university system and, more generally, to redistribute income and power to the benefit of the ruling classes.

This book was organised in three chapters, which were each developed in three steps in a long-term historical pattern (1970–2013): the construction of the alarmism, the theoretical debate and the policies implemented.

In the first chapter, I dealt with the "alarmism" on inflation, which started in the 1970s and the economic policies aimed to fight it. I showed that after the great wave of industrial action in that decade and the unions' subsequent defeat due to the decentralising of production in small units and the elimination of the automatic indexation wage mechanism, union density started to decline, and so did the wage share. After showing the CGIL's positions on the 1992 and 1993 tripartite agreements that eliminated wage indexation and promoted a new bargaining system, I dedicated a specific section to the CGIL's proposals for the economic development.

In the second chapter, I dealt with the effects of the reforms of the labour market on the employment rate and the path of labour productivity. I emphasised the gap between the expected outcomes of labour reforms and their actual outcomes. In particular, based on official evidence, I deem that (i) elimination of automatic wage indexation mechanism; (ii) the promotion of a decentralised bargaining system and (iii) labour market flexibilisation acted as the three main components of a whole-wage moderation policy, which contributed to the Italian economic decline.

In the third chapter, I dealt with the reforms of the Italian university system. Also, in this case, I focused on the gap between the expected outcome and the actual outcome. Moreover, I dedicated a specific section to the emotional health of the PhD students in Italy, showing how the competitive pressure can negatively affect their lives and performances. I concluded with a section discussing an option of economic policy, based on the view that a massive State intervention for promoting innovations (both in the public and the private sector) could be useful in reducing the unemployment rate and stimulating economic growth, via the increase of domestic demand in a short-run perspective, and could have positive outcomes on the long-run path of labour productivity.

The main conclusions are that: (i) the Italian economic stagnation is largely self-inflicted; (ii) it mainly depends on the attempt to generate economic growth by means of wage moderation. As shown, the long-term strategy of wage moderation has produced three negative effects on the rate of growth: first, it reduced domestic demand; second, it negatively affected the path of labour productivity; third, the expansion of net exports it generated did not compensate for the fall in domestic demand. At the same time, a wage moderation strategy was difficult to oppose, both on the part of unions and on the part of the government. In the first case, this occurred because Italian unions began to dramatically lose their political power from the 1980s. In the second case, this occurred because the Italian Governments were unable to counteract firms' interest in staying competitive via wage cutting. In this respect, the government did not intervene to avoid problems of lack of coordination and the firms' short-sightedness. The final part of the book dealt with this issue, proposing a long-term strategy where the State acts as innovator of the first resort.

Bibliography

Abete, L. 1996. *Mercato Sviluppo Solidarietà. 1992–1996: quattro anni di Presidenza Confindustria*, Roma, SIPI

ADI. 2019. VIII Indagine ADI su Dottorato e Post-Doc, *dottorato.it*, https:// dottorato.it/content/indagine-adi-2019

Agasisti, T., Barra, C., and Zotti, R. 2019. Research, knowledge transfer, and innovation: The effect of Italian universities' efficiency on local economic development 2006–2012, *Journal of Regional Science*, vol. 59, no. 5, 819–49

Agnello Modica, P. 2004. Contro la rendita, *Rassegna Sindacale*, no. 23, 9

Agostini, L. 1992. La parola all'assemblea dei delegati, *Rassegna Sindacale*, vol. 5, 33–34

Aidt, T. S. and Tzannatos, Z. 2008. Trade unions, collective bargaining and macroeconomic performance: A review, *Industrial Relations Journal*, vol. 39, no. 4, 258–95

Aina, C. and Casalone, G. 2018. L'abbandono degli studi universitari, *Economia & Lavoro*, vol. 2, 131–48

Alberti, M. 2016. *Senza lavoro. La disoccupazione in Italia dall'Unità a oggi*, Roma-Bari, Laterza

Alesina, A., Favero, C., and Giavazzi, F. 2019. *Austerità. Quando funziona e quando no*, Milano, Rizzoli

Alleva, P. 1992. La macchina della verità, *Rassegna Sindacale*, vol. 7, 7

Altieri, G. and Ferrucci, G. 2009. Dalla disoccupazione al lavoro flessibile: l'evoluzione del mercato del lavoro italiano, pp. 39–88, in Altieri, G. (ed.), *Un mercato del lavoro atipico. Storie ed effetti della flessibilità in Italia*, Roma, Ediesse

AMECO. *AMECO Database*, https://ec.europa.eu/info/business-economy-euro/ indicators-statistics/economic-databases/macro-economic-database-ameco/ ameco-database_en

Andreatta, B., Ciampi, C. A., Draghi, M., Grassini, F. A., Letta, E., Monti, M., Mussari, G., and Salvemini, M. T. 2011. *L'autonomia della politica monetaria. Il divorzio Tesoro-Banca d'Italia trent'anni dopo*, Bologna, Il Mulino

Antonioli, D. and Pini, P. 2013. Contrattazione, dinamica salariale e produttività: ripensare gli obiettivi ed i metodi, *Quaderni di Rassegna Sindacale*, vol. 2

Aresu, A. 2017. Una Repubblica fondata sul risparmio, *Limes*, vol. 4, 101–10

Arrigo, G. 2012. A flexibilidade do trabalho ao 'molho' italiano, pp. 123–42, in Pinheiro, R., Portela, S., and Melleiro, W. (eds.), *Relações de trabalho*. *Cenários e desafios*, São Paulo, Fundação Friedrich Ebert – Central Única dos Trabalhadores

Arrow, K. 1962. The economic implications of learning by doing, *The Review of Economic Studies*, vol. 29, no. 3, 155–73

Artoni, R. 2007. Valutazione della ricerca e pluralismo in economia politica, *Rivista Italiana degli Economisti*, vol. 2, 191–203

Baccaro, L. and Howell, C. 2017. Unhinged: Industrial relations liberalization and capitalist instability, *MPIfG Discussion Paper*, vol. 19, September, 1–24

Baccaro, L. and Pulignano, V. 2011. Employment relations in Italy, pp. 138–68, in Nick, W., Greg, B., and Lansbury, R. (eds.), *International and Comparative Employment Relations. Globalisation and the Developed Market Economies*. *5th edition*, London, Sage

Baccaro, L. and Tober, T. 2017. The role of cost and price competitiveness in the Eurozone, 10.13140/RG.2.2.32617.39528

Bagnai, A. 2016a. *Il tramonto dell'euro. Come e perché la fine della moneta unica salverebbe democrazia e benessere in Europa*, Reggio Emilia, Imprimatur

Bagnai, A. 2016b. Italy's decline and the balance-of-payments constraint: A multi-country analysis, *International Review of Applied Economics*, vol. 30, no. 1, 1–26

Bagnasco, A. 1977. *Tre Italie. La problematica territoriale dello sviluppo italiano*, Studi e ricerche, Bologna, Il Mulino

Banca d'Italia. 2018. *Economie regionali. L'economia delle regioni italiane. Dinamiche recenti e aspetti strutturali* (A. D'Ignazio and C. Rossi, Eds.), Roma, Banca d'Italia

Barbacetto, G., Gomez, P., and Travaglio, M. 2012. *Mani pulite. La vera storia, 20 anni dopo*, Milano, Chiarelettere

Barbagallo, F. 2009. *L'Italia repubblicana. Dallo sviluppo alle riforme mancate (1945–2008)*, Roma, Carocci

Barrecheguren, P. 2018. Tesis doctoral es perjudicial para la salud mental, *El País*

Becker, G. S. 1964. *Human Capital. A Theoretical and Empirical Analysis, with Special Reference to Education*, Chicago, University of Chicago Press

Bellanca, N. 2018. Quale politica economica può fronteggiare il declino italiano? *MicroMega*, http://temi.repubblica.it/micromega-online/quale-politica-economica-puo-fronteggiare-il-declino-italiano/

Bellofiore, R. 2001. I lunghi anni Settanta. Crisi sociale e integrazione economica internazionale, in Baldissara, L. (ed.), *Le radici della crisi. L'Italia tra gli anni Sessanta e Settanta*, Roma, Carocci

Bellofiore, R. 2013. L'eccezione esemplare: il caso italiano nella crisi globale ed europea, *Critica Marxista*, vol. 2, 31–42

Bellofiore, R. 2018a. La nuova università. Supermarket delle competenze, pp. 3–11, in Bellofiore, R. and Vertova, G. (eds.), *Ai confini della docenza. Per la critica dell'Università*, Torino, Accademia University Press

Bellofiore, R. 2018b. Undici tesi sull'economia politica e su Rethinking Economics: la storia del pensiero economico, la tradizione italiana e le giovani generazioni, pp. 115–28, in Bellofiore, R. and Vertova, G. (eds.), *Ai confini della docenza. Per la critica dell'Università*, Torino, Academia University Press

Bellofiore, R. 2019. Le contraddizioni delle soluzioni 'keynesiane' del problema della disoccupazione e la sfida del 'piano del lavoro', pp. 17–27, in Foggi, J. (ed.), *Tornare al lavoro*. *Lavoro di cittadinanza e piena occupazione*, Roma, Castelvecchi

Bellofiore, R. and Vertova, G. 2014. Neoliberismo, ecosistema e sistemi nazionali di innovazione: verso uno Stato innovatore di prima istanza, *La Rivista delle Scienze Sociali*, vol. 4, 211–21

Bellofiore, R. and Vertova, G. 2018. Per una critica della valutazione, pp. 41–43, in Bellofiore, R. and Vertova, G. (eds.), *Ai confini della docenza. Per la critica dell'Università*, Torino, Accademia University Press

Beltratti, A. 2007. Ricerca e didattica: valutazione ed incentivi, *Rivista Italiana degli Economisti*, vol. 2, 205–14

Benvenuto, G. and Maglie, A. 2016. *Il divorzio di San Valentino*, Roma, Bibliotheka Edizioni

Bernaciak, M., Gumbell-McCormic, R., and Hyman, R. 2015. *El sindicalismo europeo: ¿de la crisis a la renovación?* Madrid, Fundación 1° de Mayo

Berta, G. 2004. Declino o metamorfosi dell'industria italiana, *Il Mulino*, vol. 53, no. 1, 77–89

Beschi, M. and Sanna, R. 2012. Una sterile austerità, *Rassegna Sindacale*, no. 46, 2

Betti, G., D'Agostino, A., and Neri, L. 2011. Educational mismatch of graduates: A multidimensional and fuzzy indicator, *Social Indicators Research*, vol. 103, no. 3, 465–80

Bevilacqua, P. 2005. *Breve storia dell'Italia meridionale. Dall'Ottocento a oggi*, Roma, Donzelli

Bhaduri, A. and Marglin, S. 1990. Unemployment and the real wage: The economic basis for contesting political ideologies, *Cambridge Journal of Economics*, vol. 14, 375–93

Bianchi, C. 2016. A reappraisal of Verdoorn's law for the Italian economy, 1951–1997, pp. 115–35, in McCombie, J., Pugno, M., and Soro, B. (eds.), *Productivity Growth and Economic Performance*, London, Palgrave Macmillan

Bianchi, P. 2013. *La rincorsa frenata. L'industria italiana dall'unità nazionale alla crisi globale*, Bologna, Il Mulino

Bianco, M. L., Contini, B., Negri, N., Ortona, G., Scacciati, F., Terna, P., and Togati, D. 2018. I pubblici dipendenti sono troppo pochi, *Bollettino Adapt*, no. 17

Birindelli, L. 2016. *Contrattazione integrativa e retribuzioni nel settore privato*, Fondazione Di Vittorio, https://www.fondazionedivittorio.it/it/contrattazione-integrativa-e-retribuzioni-nel-settore-privato

Birindelli, L. 2019. *Retribuzioni e mercato del lavoro: l'Italia a confronto con le maggiori economie dell'Eurozona*, Fondazione Di Vittorio, https://www.fondazione divittorio.it/it/retribuzioni-e-mercato-del-lavoro-l%E2%80%99italia-confronto-maggiori-economie-dell%E2%80%80%99eurozona

Blanchard, O. 2007. A review of Richard Layard, Stephen Nickell, and Richard Jackman's unemployment: Macroeconomic performance and the labour market, *Journal of Economic Literature*, vol. 45, no. 2, 410–18

Blanchard, O. and Giavazzi, F. 2003. Macroeconomic effects of regulation and deregulation in goods and labor markets, *The Quarterly Journal of Economics*, August, 879–908

Boeri, T. and Checchi, D. 2001. Recenti tendenze del sindacato in Europa: la forbice fra presenza e influenza, in Ninni, A., Silva, F., and Vaccà, S. (eds.), *Evoluzione del lavoro, crisi del sindacato e sviluppo del paese*, Milano, Franco Angeli

Boeri, T., Faini, R., Ichino, A., Pisauro, G., and Scarpa, C. 2005. *Oltre il declino*, Bologna, Il Mulino

Borrelli, D. 2015. *Contro l'ideologia della valutazione. L'ANVUR e l'arte della rottamazione dell'università*, Sesto San Giovanni, Jouvence

Bowles, S. and Boyer, R. 1995. Wages, aggregate demand, and employment in an open economy: An empirical investigation, pp. 143–71, in Epstein, G. A. and Gintis, H. M. (eds.), *Macroeconomic Policy after the Conservative Era: Studies in Investment, Saving and Finance*, Cambridge, Cambridge University Press

Bowles, S. and Gintis, H. 1976. *Schooling in Capitalist America. Educational Reform and the Contradictions of Economic Life*, New York, Basic Books

Brancaccio, E., Garbellini, N., and Giammetti, R. 2018. Structural labour market reforms, GDP growth and the functional distribution of income, *Structural Change and Economic Dynamics*, vol. 44, 34–45

Braverman, H. 1998. *Labor and Monopoly Capital. The Degradation of Work in the Twentieth Century*, New York, New York University Press

Bronzini, R., Cannari, L., Staderini, A., Conti, L., D'Aurizio, L., Fabbrini, A., Filippone, A., Ilardi, G., Iuzzolino, G., Montanaro, P., Paccagnella, M., Pellegrini, V., and Santioni, e R. 2013. L'industria meridionale e la crisi, *Questioni di Economia e Finanza*, vol. 194

Brynjolfsson, E. and McAfee, A. 2014. *The Second Machine Age: Work, Progress, and Prosperity in a Time of Brilliant Technologies*, New York, W. W. Norton & Company

Bugamelli, M., Cannari, L., Lotti, F., and Magri, S. 2012. Il gap innovativo del sistema produttivo italiano: radici e possibili rimedi, *Questioni di Economia e Finanza*, vol. 121

Bugamelli, M., Lotti, F., Amici, M., Ciapanna, E., Colonna, F., D'Amuri, F., Giacomelli, S., Linarello, A., Manaresi, F., Palumbo, G., Scocciani, F., and Sette, E. 2018. Productivity growth in Italy: A tale of a slow-motion change, *Questioni di Economia e Finanza*, vol. 422

Caffè, F. 1972. La strategia dell'allarmismo economico, *Giornale degli Economisti e Annali di Economia, Nuova Serie*, vol. 9/10, 692–99

Caffè, F. 1990. *La solitudine del riformista* (N. Acocella and M. Franzini, Eds.), Torino, Bollati Boringhieri

Calmfors, L. and Driffill, J. 1988. Bargaining structure, corporatism and macroeconomic performance, *Economic Policy*, vol. 6, 14–61

Calvo, G. A. 1981. *On the Inefficiency of Unemployment*, New York, Columbia University

Camusso, S., Baseotto, N., Nicolosi, N., and Vanacore, G. 2003. Quella strana concezione dell'unità della CGIL, *Rassegna Sindacale*, no. 28, 4

Carniti, P. 2019. *Passato prossimo. Memorie di un sindacalista d'assalto (1973–1985)*, Roma, Castelvecchi

Carrieri, M. 1991. La montagna e il topolino, *Rassegna Sindacale*, no. 46, 9

Casalone, G. and Checchi, D. 2017. L'istruzione pubblica alla luce delle recenti riforme, in Arachi, G. and Baldini, M. (eds.), *La finanza pubblica italiana*, Bologna, Il Mulino

Castronovo, V. 2013. *Storia economica d'Italia. Dall'Ottocento ai giorni nostri*, Torino, Einaudi

Cella, G. P. 2004. *Il sindacato*, Roma-Bari, Laterza

CENSIS. 2019. *53° Rapporto sulla situazione sociale del Paese*, Milano, Franco Angeli

Cersosimo, D., Ferrara, A. R., and Nisticò, R. 2016. La mobilità geografica: da Sud a Nord senza ritorno, pp. 115–37, in Viesti, G. (ed.), *Università in declino*, Roma, Donzelli

CGIL. 2006. XV Congresso Nazionale. *Riprogettare il Paese – Lavoro, Saperi, Diritti, Libertà*

CGIL. 2010. XVI Congresso Nazionale. *I diritti e il lavoro oltre la crisi*

CGIL. 2013. Piano del Lavoro. *Creare lavoro per dare futuro e sviluppo al Paese*

Checchi, D. and Pagani, L. 2005. The effects of unions on wage inequality. The Italian case in the 1990s, *Politica Economica*, vol. 1, 43–70

Checchi, D. and Visser, J. 2005. Pattern persistence in European trade union density, *European Sociological Review*, vol. 21, no. 1, 1–22

Ciccarone, G. and Messori, M. 2013. Per la produttività programmata, *Economia & Lavoro*, vol. 3, 26–32

Ciocca, P. 2003. L'economia italiana: un problema di crescita, in *44a Riunione Scientifica Annuale*, Società Italiana degli Economisti, Salerno, 25 ottobre

Clance, P. R. and Imes, S. A. 1978. The impostor phenomenon in high achieving women: Dynamics and therapeutic intervention, *Psychotherapy: Theory, Research And Practice*, vol. 15, no. 3, 241–47

Coin, F. 2019. *L'età dell'inadeguatezza: il burnout nel mondo della ricerca*, che-Fare, www.che-fare.com/eta-inadeguatezza-burnout-ricerca-francesca-coin/

Colacchio, G. 2014. Taxation, income redistribution and debt dynamics in a seven-equation model of the business cycle, *Journal of Economic Behavior & Organization*, vol. 106, 140–65

Colacchio, G. and Forges Davanzati, G. 2017. Endogenous money, increasing returns and economic growth: Nicholas Kaldor's contribution, *Structural Change and Economic Dynamics,* vol. 41, 79–85

Colacchio, G. and Forges Davanzati, G. 2019a. Il salario come variabile indipendente: 'compatibilisti' e 'contrattualisti', *Alternative per il Socialismo*, vol. 55, 173–88

Colacchio, G. and Forges Davanzati, G. 2019b. *Modern Money Theory: A Critical Assessment and a Proposal for the State as Innovator of First Resort*, Cambridge Centre for Economic and Public Policy (CCEPP) WP02–19

Cristilli, C. 2011. Tutti i guasti del modello Penelope, *Rassegna Sindacale*, no. 12, 13

Crouch, C. 2000. The snakes and ladders of the Twenty-First century trade unionism, *Oxford Review of Economic Policy*, vol. 16, no. 1, 70–83

Crouch, C. 2009. Privatised Keynesianism: An unacknowledged policy regime, *The British Journal of Politics and International Relations*, vol. 11, 382–99

Crouch, C. 2017. Membership density and trade union power, *Transfer: European Review of Labour and Research*, vol. 23, no. 1, 47–61

Crucianelli, F. 1992. Primo: Semplificare, *Rassegna Sindacale*, nos. 1–2, 10–11

Curtarelli, M. and Gualtieri, V. 2011. Educational mismatch e qualità del lavoro: un quadro d'insieme e alcune specificità del caso italiano, *Economia & Lavoro*, vol. 3, 27–50

Dacrema, F. 2008. Come uscire dal circolo vizioso del declino, *Rassegna Sindacale*, no. 25, 14

Dal Lago, M. 2018. L'ideologia dell'occupabilità nella ristrutturazione neoliberista dei sistemi formativi, pp. 72–84, in Bellofiore, R. and Vertova, G. (eds.), *Ai confini della docenza. Per la critica dell'Università*, Torino, Accademia University Press

D'Amuri, F. and Giorgiantonio, C. 2015. Stato dell'arte e prospettive della contrattazione aziendale in Italia, *Wp Csdle "Massimo D'Antona"*

D'Antonio, M. 2013. *La crisi dell'economia italiana. Cause, responsabilità, vie d'uscita*, Soveria Mannelli, Rubbettino

Daveri, F., Jona-Lasinio, C., and Zollino, F. 2005. Italy's decline: Getting the facts right, *Giornale degli Economisti e Annali di Economia*, vol. 64, no. 4, 365–410

De Cecco, M. 2012. Una crisi lunga mezzo secolo: le cause profonde del declino italiano, *Economia Italiana*, vol. 3, 69–92

Deleidi, M. and Paternesi Meloni, W. 2019. Produttività e domanda aggregata: una verifica della legge di Kaldor-Verdoorn per l'economia italiana, *Economia & Lavoro*, vol. 2, 25–44

Del Fattore, S. 2003. Alla fine la carità dello Stato, *Rassegna Sindacale*, no. 31, 1–2

Dell'Aringa, C. and Pagani, L. 2007. Collective bargaining and wage dispersion in Europe, *British Journal of Industrial Relations*, vol. 45, no. 1, 29–54

De Luca, M. 2013. *Nel rispetto dei reciproci ruoli. Lineamenti di storia della contrattazione collettiva in Italia.*, Milano, Vita e Pensiero

Di Bartolomeo, G. and Papa, S. 2017. I sindacati come attori della politica macroeconomica, *Economia & Lavoro*, vol. 3, 13–26

D'Ippoliti, C. and Roncaglia, A. 2011. L'Italia: una crisi nella crisi, *Moneta e Credito*, vol. 64, no. 255, 189–227

Dubini, P. 2019. *Con la cultura non si mangia (falso!)*, Roma-Bari, Laterza

Dutt, A. K. 2012. Distributional dynamics in Post Keynesian growth models, *Journal of Post Keynesian Economics*, vol. 34, no. 3, 431–52

Epifani, G. 2002. E l'Italia scende in piazza per l'Italia, *Rassegna Sindacale*, no. 38, 1–2

EUROSTAT. *EUROSTAT Database*, https://ec.europa.eu/eurostat/data/database

EUROSTAT. 2018. *Population Aged 30–34 with Tertiary Educational Attainment (ISCED 5–8)*, Educational Attainment Statistics, https://ec.europa.eu/eurostat/statistics-explained/index.php/Educational_attainment_statistics

Evans, T. M., Bira, L., Gastelum, J. B., Weiss, L. T., and Vanderford, N. L. 2018. Evidence for a mental health crisis in graduate education, *Nature Biotechnology*, vol. 36, 282

Fadda, S. 2009. La riforma della contrattazione: un rischio e una proposta circa il secondo livello, *nelmerito.com*, www.nelmerito.com/index.php?option=com_content&task=view&id=759&Itemid=135

Faini, R. and Sapir, A. 2005. Un modello obsoleto? Crescita e specializzazione dell'economia italiana, pp. 19–81, in Boeri, T., Faini, R., Ichino, A., Pisauro, G., and Scarpa, C. (eds.), *Oltre il declino*, Bologna, Il Mulino

Fammoni, F. 2006. Parte la campagna 'Il rosso contro il nero', *Rassegna Sindacale*, no. 17, 1–2

Fauri, F. 2006. *L'integrazione economica europea (1947–2006)*, Bologna, Il Mulino

Felettigh, A. and Federico, S. 2011. Measuring the price elasticity of import demand in the destination markets of Italian exports, *Economia e Politica Industriale*, vol. 38, no. 1, 127–62

Felice, E. 2015. *Ascesa e declino. Storia economica d'Italia*, Bologna, Il Mulino

Ferrucci, G. 2012. *Gli effetti della crisi sul lavoro in Italia: Fondazione Di Vittorio*, https://www.fondazionedivittorio.it/it/effetti-della-crisi-sul-lavoro-italia

Ferrucci, G. 2013. *Gli effetti della crisi sul lavoro in Italia: Fondazione Di Vittorio*, https://www.fondazionedivittorio.it/it/effetti-della-crisi-sul-lavoro-italia-primo-semestre-2013

Fisher, I. 1933. The debt-deflation theory of great depressions, *Econometrica*, vol. 1, no. 4, 337–57

Flanagan, R. J. 1999. Macroeconomic performance and collective bargaining: An international perspective, *Journal of Economic Literature*, vol. 37, no. 3, 1150–75

Flisi, S., Goglio, V., Meroni, E. C., Rodrigues, M., and Vera-Toscano, E. 2017. Measuring occupational mismatch: Overeducation and overskill in Europe – evidence from PIAAC, *Social Indicators Research*, vol. 131, 1211–49

Florio, M. 2014. The return of public enterprise, Centre for Industrial Studies 1, https://ssrn.com/abstract=2563560

Foa, V. 1996. *Questo Novecento*, Torino, Einaudi

Fondazione Di Vittorio and Funzione Pubblica CGIL. 2018. *Piano straordinario per l'occupazione nelle pubbliche amministrazioni*, www.fpcgil.it/wp-content/uploads/2018/11/Piano_straordinario_occupazione.pdf

Fondazione Migrantes. 2019. *Rapporto Italiani nel Mondo (XIV edizione)*, https://www.migrantes.it/rapporto-italiani-nel-mondo-2019/

Fondazione Res. 2016. *Università in declino* (G. Viesti, Ed.), Roma, Donzelli

Forges Davanzati, G. 2002. Wages fund, high wages, and social conflict in a classical model of unemployment equilibrium, *Review of Radical Political Economics*, vol. 34, 463–86

Forges Davanzati, G. 2006. *Ethical Codes and Income Distribution. A Study of John Bates Clark and Thorstein Veblen*, London, Routledge

Forges Davanzati, G. 2011. Income distribution and crisis in a Marxian schema of the monetary circuit, *International Journal of Political Economy*, vol. 40, no. 3, 33–49

Forges Davanzati, G. 2013. Gunnar Myrdal on labour market regulation and economic development, *Œconomia – History, Methodology, Philosophy*, vol. 3, no. 1, 3–21

Forges Davanzati, G. 2015. Nicholas Kaldor on endogenous money and increasing returns, *Post Keynesian Economics Study Group Working*, vol. WP 1505, 1–16

Forges Davanzati, G. 2016. Alle origini del declino economico italiano. Domanda aggregata, dimensioni d'impresa e sottofinanziamento dell'Università, *Itinerari di ricerca storica*, vol. XXX, no. 1 (nuova serie)

90   Bibliography

Forges Davanzati, G. 2018. High wages and economic growth in a Kaldorian theoretical framework, in Gabellini, T., Gasperin, S., and Moneta, A. (eds.), *Economic
Crisis and Economic Thought: Alternative Theoretical Perspectives on the Economic Crisis*, London, Routledge

Forges Davanzati, G. and Giangrande, N. 2017a. Gli effetti della contrattazione
decentrata su salari e produttività del lavoro, *Quaderni di Rassegna Sindacale*,
vol. 4, 155–79

Forges Davanzati, G. and Giangrande, N. 2017b. Le politiche del lavoro e formative
in Italia (2008–2015): un'analisi critica, pp. 173–211, in Di Maio, A. and Marani,
U. (eds.), *Politiche economiche e crisi internazionale. Uno sguardo sull'Europa*,
Roma, L'Asino d'oro

Forges Davanzati, G. and Giangrande, N. 2019a. A crise econômica italiana e a
proposta do Estado como inovador de primeira instância, *Revista Brasileira
De Economia Social E Do Trabalho*, vol. 1, no. e019004, 1–22, https://doi.
org/10.20396/rbest.v1i0.12657

Forges Davanzati, G. and Giangrande, N. 2019b. Il declino inevitabile, se lo
Stato non innova, *Huffington Post*, https://www.huffingtonpost.it/entry/
il-declino-inevitabile-se-lo-stato-non-innova_it_5cf8db50e4b0638bdfa4f26c

Forges Davanzati, G. and Giangrande, N. 2019c. Labour market deregulation, taxation and labour productivity in a Marxian – Kaldorian perspective: The case
of Italy, *Cambridge Journal of Economics*, vol. 44, no. 2, 371–390, https://doi.
org/10.1093/cje/bez041

Forges Davanzati, G. and Giangrande, N. 2019d. The theoretical basis of the CGIL's
analysis of the Italian economic decline, *Brazilian Keynesian Review*, vol. 5, no.
1, 126–53

Forges Davanzati, G. and Mongelli, L. 2018. Does rising unemployment lead to
policies of labour flexibility? The Italian case (1990–2013), *Economia & Lavoro*,
vol. 3, 15–28

Forges Davanzati, G. and Pacella, A. 2010. Emulation, indebtedness and income
distribution. A monetary theory of production approach, *Intervention – European
Journal of Economics and Economic Policies,* vol. 7, no. 1, 145–65

Forges Davanzati, G., Pacella, A., and Salento, A. 2019. Financialisation in context:
The case of Italy, *Cambridge Journal of Economics*, vol. 43, no. 4, 917–36

Forges Davanzati, G. and Patalano, R. 2015. The economics of high wages and the
policy implications: The case of Francesco Saverio Nitti, *History of Economic
Ideas*, vol. 23, no. 2, 73–98

Forges Davanzati, G., Patalano, R., and Traficante, G. 2017. The Italian economic
stagnation in a Kaldorian theoretical perspective, *Economia Politica*, 1–21

Forges Davanzati, G. and Paulì, G. 2015. Il mito della spesa pubblica come spreco:
il caso italiano, pp. 123–56, in Di Maio, A. and Marani, U. (eds.), *Economia e
luoghi comuni. Convenzioni, retorica e riti*, Roma, L'Asino d'oro

Franzina, E. 2003. *Traversate. Le grandi migrazioni transatlantiche e i racconti
italiani del viaggio per mare*, Foligno, Editoriale Umbra

Franzini, M. and Pianta, M. 2016. *Disuguaglianze. Quante sono, come combatterle*,
Roma-Bari, Editori Laterza

Freeman, R. B. 1976. *The overeducated American*, New York, Academic Press

Galantini, E. 1991. Il fondo del negoziato, *Rassegna Sindacale*, no. 45, 10–11

Galli, G. 2004. *I partiti politici italiani (1943–2004)*, Milano, Rizzoli

Gallino, L. 1998. *Se tre milioni vi sembran pochi. Sui modi per combattere la disoccupazione*, Torino, Einaudi

Gallino, L. 2003. *La scomparsa dell'Italia industriale*, Vele (Torino), Torino, Einaudi

Gallino, L. 2012. *La lotta di classe dopo la lotta di classe* (P. Borgna, Ed.), Roma-Bari, Laterza

Gallino, L. 2014. *Vite rinviate. Lo scandalo del lavoro precario*, Roma-Bari, Laterza

Gambarotto, F. and Solari, S. 2014. The peripheralization of Southern European capitalism within the EMU, *Review of International Political Economy*, vol. 22, no. 4, 788–812

Garegnani, P. 2007. Sulla valutazione della ricerca economica, *Rivista Italiana degli Economisti*, vol. 2, 177–90

Garruccio, R. 2005. Un sistema sotto sforzo. L'ipotesi del declino industriale italiano, *Contemporanea*, vol. 8, no. 1, 173–83

Giangrande, N. 2016. *As posições, as propostas e as ações da CGIL para combater o desemprego na Itália (2004–2013)*, Universidade Estadual de Campinas, SP, Brasil

Giangrande, N. 2019a. *L'Università italiana nuoce gravemente alla salute emotiva dei giovani accademici?*, Paper presented on 29 May 2019 at the annual PhD workshop of the Department of History, Society and Human Studies at the University of Salento, Lecce (unpublished manuscript)

Giangrande, N. 2019b. Rilanciare lo sviluppo: occupazione e politiche industriali, pp. 125–42, in *Dieci idee per ripensare il capitalismo*, Milano, Fondazione Giangiacomo Feltrinelli

Giangrande, N. 2019c. *Una breve nota sul declino economico italiano: la moderazione salariale*, Fondazione Giangiacomo Feltrinelli, http://fondazionefeltrinelli.it/una-breve-nota-sul-declino-economico-italiano-la-moderazione-salariale/

Giavazzi, F. 2013. La ragnatela corporativa, *Corriere della Sera*

Gigliobianco, A. and Toniolo, G. (eds.). 2017. *Concorrenza, mercato e crescita in Italia: il lungo periodo*, Padova, Marsilio

Ginsborg, P. 2006. *Storia d'Italia dal dopoguerra a oggi*, Torino, Einaudi

Giunta, A. and Rossi, S. 2017. *Che cosa sa fare l'Italia. La nostra economia dopo la grande crisi*, Roma-Bari, Laterza

Gomellini, M. and Pianta, M. 2007. Commercio con l'estero e tecnologia in Italia negli anni Cinquanta e Sessanta, pp. 359–594, in Antonelli, C., Barbiellini Amidei, F., Giannetti, R., Gomellini, M., Pastorelli, S., and Pianta, M. (eds.), *Innovazione tecnologica e sviluppo industriale nel secondo dopoguerra*, Roma-Bari, Laterza

Graziani, A. 1989. The theory of the monetary circuit, *Thames Papers in Political Economy*, 1–26

Graziani, A. 1997. *I conti senza l'oste. Quindici anni di economia italiana*, Torino, Bollati Boringhieri

Graziani, A. 2000. *Lo sviluppo dell'economia italiana. Dalla ricostruzione alla moneta europea*, Torino, Bollati Boringhieri

Grilli, J. and Allesina, S. 2017. Last name analysis of mobility, gender imbalance, and nepotism across academic systems, *PNAS*, vol. 114, no. 29, 7600–5

Gros, D. and Thygesen, N. 1992. *European Monetary Integration: From the European Monetary System to European Monetary Union*, London-New York, Addison-Wesley Longman Ltd

Grüning, B. and Russo, T. 2018. Stesso lavoro, stessi diritti, Perché noi no? *FLC-CGIL*, www.flcgil.it/files/pdf/20181029/indagine-precariato-universitario-stesso-lavoro-stessi diritti-perche-noi-no-2018.pdf

Guzzonato, M. 2003. Dieci milioni di ragioni per andare avanti, *Rassegna Sindacale*, no. 40, 1–2

Halevi, J. 2018. *The Political Economy of Europe since 1945. A Kaleckian Perspective*, Advance Access published 2018, Working Paper

Hein, E. 2017. The Bhaduri-Marglin post-Kaleckian model in the history of distribution and growth theories: An assessment by means of model closures, *Review of Keynesian Economics*, vol. 5, no. 2, 218–38

Hout, M. 2012. Social and economic returns to college education in the United States, *Annual Review of Sociology*, vol. 38, 379–400

Hyman, R. 2001. *Understanding European Trade Unionism. Between Market, Class and Society*, London, Sage

Ichino, A., Gagliarducci, S., Peri, G., and Perotti, R. 2005. Lo splendido isolamento dell'università italiana, pp. 157–219, in Boeri, T., Faini, R., Ichino, A., Pisauro, G., and Scarpa, C. (eds.), *Oltre il declino*, Bologna, Il Mulino

Ichino, A., Mealli, F., and Nannicini, T. 2004. *Il lavoro interinale in Italia: trappola del precariato o trampolino verso un impiego stabile?* Pisa, Università di Pisa

ISTAT. *I.Stat Database*, http://dati.istat.it/

ISTAT. 2014. *Struttura e dimensione delle Imprese – Archivio Statistico delle Imprese Attive (ASIA)*, www.istat.it/it/archivio/131578

ISTAT. 2018. Mobilità interna e migrazioni internazionali della popolazione residente, *Anno 2017*, www.istat.it/it/files/2018/12/Report-Migrazioni-Anno-2017.pdf

ISTAT. 2019. Bilancio demografico nazionale, *Anno 2018*, https://www.istat.it/it/archivio/231884

Jessop, B. 2007. What follows Neo-liberalism? The deepening contradictions of US domination and the struggle for a new global order, pp. 67–88, in Albritton, R., Jessop, B., and Westra, R. (eds.), *Political Economy and Global Capitalism: The 21st Century, Present and Future*, London, Anthem Press

Kaldor, N. 1955. Alternative theories of distribution, *The Review of Economic Studies*, vol. 23, no. 2, 83

Kaldor, N. 1966. *Causes of the Slow Rate of Economic Growth of the United Kingdom. An Inaugural Lecture*, Cambridge, Cambridge University Press

Kaldor, N. 1981. *The Role of Increasing Returns, Technical Progress and Cumulative Causation in the Theory of International Trade and Economic Growth*, Économie appliquée

Kaldor, N. 1989. *Further Essays on Economic Theory and Policy* (A. P. Thirlwall and F. Targetti, Eds.), London, Duckworth

Kalecki, M. 1943. Political aspects of full employment, *The Political Quarterly*, vol. 14, no. 4, 322–30

Kalecki, M. 1968. The Marxian equations of reproduction and modern economics, *Social Science Information*, vol. 7, no. 6, 73–79

Kalecki, M. 1971. Class struggle and the distribution of national income, *Kyklos*, vol. 24, no. 1, 1–9

Kleinknecht, A. 2015. How 'structural reforms' of labour markets harm innovation, Research Paper

Krämer, H. M. 2011. Bowley's law: The diffusion of an empirical supposition into economic theory, *Cahiers d'économie politique/Papers in Political Economy*, vol. 61, 19–49

Kriesler, P. and Halevi, J. 2001. Political aspects of 'buffer stock employment', pp. 72–82, in Carlson, E. and Mitchell, W. F. (eds.), *Achieving Full Employment, Supplement to The Economic and Labour Relations Review, Volume 12*

Lampa, R. and Perri, S. 2014. Il declino e la crisi dell'economia italiana: dalla teoria ai fatti stilizzati, in Cerqueti, R. (ed.), *Polymorphic Crisis. Readings on the Great Recession of the 21st Century*, Macerata, EUM

Landini, F. 2017. Metamorfosi istituzionale ed eterogeneità delle imprese: all'origine della bassa crescita italiana, *Il Menabò di Etica ed Economia*, www.eticaeconomia.it/metamorfosi-istituzionale-ed-eterogeneita-delle-imprese-allorigine-della-bassa-crescita-italiana/

Lapadula, B. 2003. Un documento vuoto, *Rassegna Sindacale*, no. 30, 3

Lapadula, B. 2004. *La scossa. Un patto tra produttori per la ripresa*, Roma, Ediesse

Lavoie, M. 2014. *Post-Keynesian Economics. New Foundations*, Cheltenham, Edward Elgar

Layard, R., Nickell, S., and Jackman, R. 1991. The macroeconomics of unemployment, in *Unemployment: Macroeconomic Performance and the Labour Market*, Oxford, Oxford University Press

Leon, P. 2008. Le politiche economiche e monetarie europee e la precarietà, pp. 35–45, in Leon, P. and Realfonzo, R. (eds.), *L'economia della precarietà*, Roma, Manifestolibri

Leon, P. 2017. *I poteri ignoranti. Ascesa e caduta dell'economia dell'accumulazione*, Roma, Castelvecchi

Leonardi, S. 2009. La flexicurity italiana: la fallita riforma degli ammortizzatori sociali, pp. 291–337, in Altieri, G. (ed.), *Un mercato del lavoro atipico. Storie ed effetti della flessibilità in Italia*, Roma, Ediesse

Leonardi, S., Ambra, M. C., and Ciarini, A. 2017. *Italian collective bargaining at a turning point, WP CSDLE 'Massimo d'Antona'* 139

Lepre, A. 2006. *Storia della prima Repubblica. L'Italia dal 1943 al 2003*, Bologna, Il Mulino

Leuven, E. and Oosterbeek, H. 2011. Overeducation and mismatch in the labor market. IZA DP 5523

Levecque, K., Anseel, F., De Beuckelaer, A., Van der Heyden, J., and Gisle, L. 2017. Work organization and mental health problems in PhD students, *Research Policy*, vol. 46, no. 4, 868–79

Lippi, M. and Peracchi, F. 2007. Il primo esercizio italiano di valutazione della ricerca: una prima valutazione, *Rivista Italiana degli Economisti*, vol. 2, 267–76

Livi Bacci, M. 2017. La demografia prima di tutto, *Limes*, vol. 4, 41–47

Lucarelli, S., Palma, D., and Romano, R. 2013. Quando gli investimenti rappresentano un vincolo. Contributo alla discussione sulla crisi italiana nella crisi internazionale, *Moneta e Credito*, vol. 67, 167–203

Lucarelli, S. and Romano, R. 2015. The Italian crisis within the European crisis. The relevance of the technological foreign constraint, *World Economic Review*, no. 6, 12–30

Lucas, R. E. 1988. On the mechanism of economic development, *Journal of Monetary Economics*, vol. 22, 3–42

Lucchese, M., Nascia, L., and Pianta, M. 2016. Una politica industriale e tecnologica per l'Italia, *Argomenti*, vol. 4, 25–50

Luciano, A. and Romanò, S. 2017. Università e lavoro. Una misura del mismatch tra istruzione e occupazione, *Scuola democratica*, vol. 2, 319–41

Lunghini, G. 2012. *Conflitto Crisi Incertezza. La teoria economica dominante e le teorie alternative*, Torino, Bollati Boringhieri

Macchiati, A. 2016. *Perché l'Italia cresce poco*, Bologna, Il Mulino

Mammarella, G. and Cacace, P. 2013. *Storia e politica dell'Unione Europea*, Roma-Bari, Laterza

Manacorda, M. 2004. Can the scala mobile explain the fall and rise of earnings inequality in Italy? A semiparametric analysis, 1977–1993, *Journal of Labor Economics*, vol. 22, no. 3, 585–613

Mascini, M. 1992. Il sindacato sulla scala mobile: 'Niente accordo? Allora la legge', *Il Sole 24 Ore, 12*

Mazzucato, M. 2014. *Lo Stato innovatore*, Roma-Bari, Laterza

McCombie, J. and Thirlwall, A. P. 1994. Export-led growth and the balance-of-payments constraint, pp. 421–56, in McCombie, J. and Thirlwall, A. P. (eds.), *Economic Growth and the Balance-of-Payments Constraint*, London, Palgrave Macmillan

McCombie, J. S. L. and Spreafico, M. R. M. 2016. Kaldor's 'technical progress function' and Verdoorn's law revisited, *Cambridge Journal of Economics*, vol. 40, no. 4, 1117–36

McGuinness, S. 2006. Overeducation in the labour market, *Journal of Economic Surveys*, vol. 20, no. 3, 387–418

Millemaci, E. and Ofria, F. 2014. Kaldor-Verdoorn's law and increasing returns to scale: A comparison across developed countries, *Journal of Economic Studies*, vol. 41, no. 1, 140–162, https://doi.org/10.1108/JES-02-2012-0026

Millemaci, E. and Ofria, F. 2016. Supply and demand-side determinants of productivity growth in Italian regions, *Structural Change and Economic Dynamics*, vol. 37, 138–46

Milone, L. M. 2005. Il declino economico dell'Italia: i termini del dibattito, *Meridiana*, vol. 54, 63–88

Ministero dell'Interno. 2019. *Archivio Storico Elezioni*, https://elezionistorico. interno.gov.it/

Minsky, H. P. 2014. *Combattere la povertà. Lavoro non assistenza* (R. Bellofiore and L. Pennacchi, Eds.), Roma, Ediesse

Morata, F. 1999. *La Unión Europea: procesos, actores y políticas*, Barcelona, Ariel

Moro, D. 2011. I perché del declino italiano, *MicroMega*, http://temi.repubblica.it/ micromega-online/i-perche-del-declino-italiano/

Moro, D. 2015. *Globalizzazione e decadenza industriale. L'Italia tra delocalizzazioni, 'crisi secolare' ed euro*, Reggio Emilia, Imprimatur

Moro, D. 2018a. L'internazionalizzazione dell'economia dell'Italia nel passaggio dalla semiperiferia al centro dell'economia-mondo, *Dialettica & Filosofia*, 1–15

Moro, D. 2018b. *La gabbia dell'euro. Perché uscirne è internazionalista e di sinistra*, Reggio Emilia, Imprimatur

Moscone, F., Tosetti, E., and Vittadini, G. 2016. The impact of precarious employment on mental health: The case of Italy, *Social Science & Medicine*, vol. 158, 86–95

Munsech-Capsada, Q. 2017. Overeducation: Concept, theories and empirical evidence, *Sociology Compass*, vol. 11, August, 1–17

Myrdal, G. 1957. *Economic theory and under-developed regions*, Harper Torchbooks, London, G. Duckworth

Nuvolari, A. and Vasta, M. 2015. The Ghost in the Attic? The Italian National Innovation System in Historical Perspective, 1861–2011, *Enterprise & Society*, vol. 16, no. 2, 270–290

O'Connor, J. 1976. *The Fiscal Crisis of the State*, New Brunswick, NJ, St. Martin's Press

OECD. *OECD.Stat Database*, https://stats.oecd.org/

OECD. 2013a. *Entrepreneurship at a Glance 2013*, Paris, OECD Publishing, http:// dx.doi.org/10.1787/entrepreneur_aag-2013-en

OECD. 2013b. *Methodology Used to Compile the OECD Indicators of Employment Protection*, https://www.oecd.org/employment/emp/oecdindicatorsofemployment protection-methodology.htm

OECD. 2017. *The Great Divergence(s): The link Between Growing Productivity Dispersion and Wage Inequality*, Directorate for Science, Technology and Innovation Policy Note, May 2017, https://www.oecd.org/sti/ind/PolicyNote_ GreatDivergences_FINAL.pdf

OECD. 2019. *Education at a Glance 2019*, https://read.oecd-ilibrary.org/education/ education-at-a-glance-2019_f8d7880d-en

Ofria, F. 2009. L'approccio Kaldor-Verdoorn: una verifica empirica per il Centro-Nord e il Mezzogiorno d'Italia (anni 1951–2006), *Rivista di Politica Economica*, vol. 1, no. 1, 179–207

Ostry, J. D., Prakash, L., and Furceri, D. 2016. Neoliberalism: Oversold? *IMF Finance & Development*, vol. 53, no. 2

Pacella, A. 2008. The effects of labour market flexibility in the monetary theory of production, *Metroeconomica*, vol. 59, no. 4, 608–32

Paolazzi, L. 2014. Italy hobbled by an inefficient public sector, *Review of Economic Conditions of Italy*, no. Italy and the Eurozone on a knife-edge, 45–60

Pasimeni, C. 2016. Prove di riforma e ruolo delle Università meridionali nel divario Nord-Sud del paese (2008–2010), *Itinerari di ricerca storica*, vol. 1

Pasinetti, L. 2008. Debito pubblico nei paesi dell'Unione Europea: due modi di affrontare il problema, *Alternative per il Socialismo*, vol. 4, 172–84

Paternesi Meloni, W. 2018. Italy's price competitiveness: An empirical assessment through export elasticities, *Italian Economic Journal*, vol. 4, no. 3, 421–62

Pellegrino, B. and Zingales, L. 2017. *Diagnosing the Italian Disease: Chicago Booth*, http://faculty.chicagobooth.edu/luigi.zingales/papers/research/Diagnosing.pdf

Pennacchi, L. 2018. Innovazione e lavoro: la cerniera umanistica tra macroeconomia e microeconomia, pp. 389–404, in Cipriani, A., Gramolati, A., and Mari, G. (eds.), *Il lavoro 4.0. La Quarta Rivoluzione industriale e le trasformazioni delle attività lavorative*, Firenze, Firenze University Press

Pepe, A., Iuso, P., and Loreto, F. 2003. *La CGIL e il Novecento italiano. Un secolo di lotte, di passioni, di proposte per i diritti e la dignità del lavoro*, Roma, Ediesse

Perri, S. 2013. Bassa domanda e declino italiano, *Economia e Politica*, www.economiaepolitica.it/primo-piano/bassa-domanda-e-declino-italiano/

Perri, S. and Lampa, R. 2017. L'inscalfibile egemonia dello spontaneismo: la "Grande Ritirata" dello stato e la crisi dell'occupazione in Italia, pp. 167–210, in Ramazzotti, P. (ed.), *Stato sociale, politica economica e democrazia. Riflessioni sullo spazio e il ruolo dell'intervento pubblico oggi*, Trieste, Asterios

Perri, S. and Lampa, R. 2018. When small-sized and non-innovating firms meet a crisis: Evidence from the Italian labour market, *PSL Quarterly Review*, vol. 71, no. 284, 61–83

Pesole, D. 2010. L'autunno nero del '92 tra tasse e svalutazioni, *Il Sole 24 Ore*

Petrini, R. 2003. *Il declino dell'Italia*, Roma-Bari, Laterza

Pianta, M. 2012. *Nove su dieci. Perché stiamo (quasi) tutti peggio di 10 anni fa*, Saggi Tascabili Laterza, Editori Laterza

Piermattei, M. 2017. Basta vivere di speranze smetto con la ricerca per vendere ricambi d'auto, *Repubblica.it*, www.repubblica.it/cronaca/2017/07/12/news/basta_vivere_di_speranze_smetto_con_la_ricerca_per_vendere_ricambi_d_auto-170579634/

Pini, P. 2015a. Il Jobs Act tra surrealismo e mistificazione: una lettura critica, *Economia & Lavoro*, vol. 2, 177–215

Pini, P. 2015b. Salari e innovazione per tornare a crescere, *Sbilanciamoci.info*, http://sbilanciamoci.info/salari-e-innovazione-per-tornare-a-crescere-29016/

Pizzorno, A., Reyneri, E., Regini, M., and Regalia, I. 1978. *Lotte operaie e sindacato: il ciclo 1968–1972 in Italia*, Bologna, Il Mulino

Pontarollo, E. 2005. Il declino economico italiano. Cause e possibili rimedi, *Aggiornamenti Sociali*, vol. 11, 691–702

Praussello, F. and Marenco, M. 1996. *Economia dell'istruzione e del capitale umano*, Roma-Bari, Laterza

Protocollo. 1991. *Protocollo d'intesa per interventi urgenti di lotta all'inflazione*

Protocollo. 1992. *Protocollo sulla politica dei redditi, la lotta all'inflazione e il costo del lavoro*

Protocollo. 1993. *Protocollo sulla politica dei redditi e dell'occupazione, sugli assetti contrattuali, sulle politiche del lavoro e sul sostegno al sistema produttivo*

Pugliese, E. and Rebeggiani, E. 2004. *Occupazione e disoccupazione in Italia. Dal dopoguerra ai giorni nostri*, Roma, Edizioni Lavoro

Raitano, M. and Supino, S. 2005. A proposito di declino: la questione del capitale umano, *Meridiana*, vol. 54, 89–117

Ramskogler, P. 2007. *Uncertainty, Market Power and Credit Rationing*, August, Advance Access published 2007, Working Paper No. 105

Rangone, M. and Solari, S. 2012. 'Southern European' capitalism and the social costs of business enterprise, *Studi e Note di Economia*, vol. 1, 3–28

Regini, M. 1981. *I dilemmi del sindacato. Conflitto e partecipazione negli anni settanta e ottanta*, Bologna, Il Mulino

Resce, M. 2018. Produttività del lavoro in Italia e misure di sostegno nella contrattazione aziendale, *Economia & Lavoro*, vol. 3, 153–78

Reyneri, E. 1995. Italia, lunga attesa al riparo della famiglia e delle garanzie pubbliche, pp. 117–34, in Benoît-Guilbot, O. and Gallie, D. (eds.), *La disoccupazione di lunga durata*, Napoli, Liguori Editore

Ricci, A. and Tronti, L. 2018. Il ruolo della contrattazione e delle istituzioni del mercato del lavoro, pp. 253–76, in Franzini, M. and Raitano, M. (eds.), *Il mercato rende diseguali? La disuguaglianza dei redditi in Italia*, Bologna, Il Mulino

ROARS. 2019. *Partono le università di serie A: saranno al Nord e le deciderà ANVUR*, https://www.roars.it/online/partono-le-universita-di-serie-a-saranno-al-norde-le-decidera-anvur/

Rocchi, N. 2006. Il vizio antico del protezionismo, *Rassegna Sindacale*, no. 12, 6

Romano, R. and Ferrari, S. 2003. Analisi e proposte. Il declino italiano in cifre, *La Rivista del Manifesto*, 19–24

Romer, P. M. 1986. Increasing returns and long-run growth, *The Journal of Political Economy*, vol. 94, no. 5, 1002–37

Romero, J. P. and McCombie, J. S. L. 2015. The multi-sectoral Thirlwall's Law: Evidence from 14 developed European Countries using product-level data: CCEPP WP 04–15

Sai, M. 1992. Una scelta sbagliata, *Rassegna Sindacale*, vols. 1–2, 19–20

Salento, A. 2016. Un neoliberismo a bassa intensità: trentacinque anni di 'riforme' in Italia, pp. 3–32, in Barbera, F., Dagnes, J., Salento, A., and Spina, F. (eds.), *Il capitale quotidiano. Un manifesto per l'economia fondamentale*, Roma, Donzelli

Salento, A. and Masino, G. 2013. *La fabbrica della crisi. Finanziarizzazione delle imprese e declino del lavoro*, Roma, Carocci

Saltari, E. and Travaglini, G. 2006. *Le radici del declino economico. Occupazione e produttività in Italia nell'ultimo decennio*, Torino, UTET

Saltini, L. 2006. Se non sai non sei: avviata la campagna di sensibilizzazione contro l'analfabetismo di ritorno, *Rassegna Sindacale*, no. 22, 8

Salvati, M. 2000. *Occasioni mancate. Economia e politica in Italia dagli anni '60 a oggi*, Roma-Bari, Laterza

Sanna, R. 2013. L'economia pubblica per il Piano del Lavoro: l'impatto macroeconomico di una nuova regolazione di nuovi investimenti pubblici e di un intervento pubblico diretto alla creazione di nuova occupazione, in Pennacchi, L. (ed.), *Tra crisi e 'grande trasformazione'. Libro bianco per il Piano del Lavoro 2013*, Roma, Ediesse

Sanna, R. 2014. L'occasione da non perdere, pp. 218–45, in Comito, V., Paci, N., and Travaglini, G. (eds.), *Un paese in bilico. L'Italia tra crisi del lavoro e vincoli dell'euro*, Roma, Ediesse

Sapelli, G. 2004. Il declino non basta, *Italianieuropei, vol.* 4

Sapelli, G. 2012. *Storia economica dell'Italia contemporanea*, Milano, Bruno Mondadori

Saracco, P. 2005. Le politiche per la ricerca e per l'innovazione: i nodi da sciogliere, al di là della retorica, *Meridiana*, vol. 54, 135–56

Sateriale, G. 1991. Così nasce un non accordo, *Rassegna Sindacale*, no. 47, 9–10

Sateriale, G. 2013. Un'impostazione dal basso, *Rassegna Sindacale*, no. 3, 4

Sbarile, A. 2018. 1992: quando svalutammo la moneta per svalutare i salari, *Keynes Blog*, https://keynesblog.com/2018/02/27/1992-quando-svalutammo-la-moneta-per-svalutare-i-salari/#more-7853

Shapiro, C. and Stiglitz, J. E. 1984. Equilibrium unemployment as a worker discipline device, *American Economic Association*, vol. 74, no. 3, 433–44

Simon, H. A. 1982. *Models of Bounded Rationality (2 vols)*, Cambridge, MIT Press

Simoni, M. 2013. Le radici del declino economico italiano, *Il Mulino*, vol. 2, 210–18

Soro, B. 2006. Postilla sul declino economico, *Materiali per una storia della cultura giuridica,* vol. 2, 521–28

Sraffa, P. 1960. *Produzione di merci a mezzo di merci*, Torino, Einaudi

Standing, G. 2011. *Precari. La nuova classe esplosiva*, Bologna, Il Mulino

Stella, G. A. and Rizzo, S. 2010. *La deriva*, Milano, Rizzoli

Stockhammer, E. and Ramskogler, P. 2008. Uncertainty and exploitation in history, *Journal of Economic Issues,* vol. 42, no. 1, 175–94

Storm, S. 2019a. *How to Ruin a Country in Three Decades*, Institute for New Economic Thinking, www.ineteconomics.org/perspectives/blog/how-to-ruin-a-country-in-three-decades

Storm, S. 2019b. Lost in Deflation: Why Italy's woes are a warning to the whole Eurozone, *International Journal of Political Economy*, vol. 48, no. 3, 195–237

Streeck, W. 1992. From national corporatism to transnational pluralism. European interest politics and the single market, pp. 97–126, in Treu, T. (ed.), *Participation in Public Policy-Making. The Role of Trade Unions and Employers' Association*, Berlin, De Gruyter

Streeck, W. 2005. The sociology of labor markets and trade unions, pp. 254–83, in Smelser, N. J. and Swedberg, R. (eds.), *The Handbook of Economic Sociology*, Princeton, Princeton University Press

Streeck, W. 2011. The crises of democratic capitalism, *New Left Review,* vol. 71, 5–29

Streeck, W. 2013. The politics of public debt: Neoliberalism, capitalist development and the restructuring of the state, *Max Planck Institute for the Study of Societies*, vol. DP 13/7, 1–24

SVIMEZ. 2019. *Rapporto SVIMEZ 2018. L'economia e la società nel Mezzogiorno*, Bologna, Il Mulino

Sylos Labini, P. 1984. *Le forze dello sviluppo e del declino*, Roma-Bari, Laterza

Sylos Labini, P. 2006. *Torniamo ai classici. Produttività del lavoro, progresso tecnico e sviluppo economico*, Roma-Bari, Laterza

Targetti, F. 1988. *Nicholas Kaldor: teoria e politica economica di un capitalismo in mutamento*, Bologna, Il Mulino

Targetti, F. 2003. Le cause del declino italiano, *Italianieuropei*, vol. 3

Toniolo, G. 2004. L'Italia verso il declino economico? Ipotesi e congetture in una prospettiva secolare, *Rivista Italiana degli Economisti*, vol. 1, 29–45

Trentin, B. 1991. Il virus della doppiezza, *Rassegna Sindacale*, no. 47, 11–13

Trentin, B. 2017. *Diari 1988–1994* (I. Ariemma, Ed.), Roma, Ediesse

Trésor-Economics. 2016. *Why is Italian Productivity so Weak?* https://www.tresor.economie.gouv.fr/Articles/2018/03/01/tresor-economics-no-170-why-is-italian-productivity-so-weak

Trichet, J.-C. and Draghi, M. 2011. Letter of ECB to Italy, *Corriere della Sera*

Tridico, P. 2009. Flessibilità e istituzioni nel mercato del lavoro: dagli economisti classici agli economisti istituzionalisti, *Economia & Lavoro*, 113–39

Tridico, P. 2012. The impact of the economic crisis on the EU labour market: A comparative perspective, Departmental Working Papers of Economics – University 'Roma Tre' 153

Tridico, P. 2014a. From economic decline to the current crisis in Italy, *International Review of Applied Economics*, vol. 29, no. 2, 164–93

Tridico, P. 2014b. Produttività, contrattazione e salario di risultato: un confronto tra l'Italia e il resto d'Europa, *Economia & Lavoro*, vol. 2, 147–70

Tridico, P. 2015. Riforme del mercato del lavoro, occupazione e produttività: un confronto tra l'Italia e l'Europa, *Sindacalismo*, vol. 28/2014, 61–92

Tridico, P. 2018. Patto per la Produttività Programmata, *Economia e Politica*, www.economiaepolitica.it/lavoro-e-diritti/lavoro-e-sindacato/patto-per-la-produttivita-programmata/

Tridico, P. and Pariboni, R. 2017. Inequality, financialization, and economic decline, *Journal of Post Keynesian Economics*, 1–24

Troffa, M. 2004. Il disegno di un'altra Italia autoritaria e plebiscitaria, *Rassegna Sindacale*, no. 21, 4

Tronti, L. 2005. Protocollo di luglio e crescita economica: l'occasione perduta, *Rivista Internazionale di Scienze Sociali*, vol. 2, 345–70

Tronti, L. 2009. La crisi di produttività dell'economia italiana: scambio politico ed estensione del mercato, *Economia & Lavoro*, vol. 2, 139–57

Tronti, L. 2010. The Italian productivity slow-down: The role of the bargaining model, *International Journal of Manpower*, vol. 31, no. 7, 770–92

Tronti, L. 2013. A mo' di conclusione: riforma della contrattazione in tre punti, *Economia & Lavoro*, vol. 3, 58–65

Tronti, L. 2016. Modello contrattuale, produttività del lavoro e crescita economica, *Quaderni di Rassegna Sindacale*, vol. 2

UDU. 2018. *Atenei fuorilegge*, https://www.unionedegliuniversitari.it/atenei-tasse-fuorilegge-dossier-2018/

Vadacchino, D. and Nardi, M. 2019. Curami! Sono un post-doc, *ROARS,* https://www.roars.it/online/curami-sono-un-post-doc/

Verdoorn, P. J. 1949. Fattori che regolano la produttività del lavoro, *L'industria,* vol. 1, 45–53

Vertova, G. 2014. *The State and National Systems of Innovation: A Sympathetic Critique*, Levy Economics Institute, Working Papers Series No. 823

Vertova, G. 2018. Una analisi della Riforma Moratti (legge 133/2008), pp. 30–40, in Bellofiore, R. and Vertova, G. (eds.), *Ai confini della docenza. Per la critica dell'Università*, Torino, Accademia University Press

Viesti, G. 2016. Il declino del sistema universitario, pp. 3–56, in Viesti, G. (ed.), *Università in declino*, Roma, Donzelli

Viesti, G. 2018. *La laurea negata. Le politiche contro l'istruzione*, Roma-Bari, Laterza

Visser, J. 2019. *J. Visser, ICTWSS Database. Version 6.1*. Amsterdam, Amsterdam Institute for Advanced Labour Studies (AIAS), University of Amsterdam. November

Wray, R. 2019. L'importanza economica e sociale della piena occupazione, pp. 33–44, in Foggi, J. (ed.), *Tornare al lavoro. Lavoro di cittadinanza e piena occupazione*, Roma, Castelvecchi

Young, M. 1958. *The Rise of the Meritocracy 1870–2033. An Essay on Education and Society*, London, Thames and Hudson

Zoppoli, L. 2011. Contrattazione collettiva e Unità d'Italia, *Wp Csdle "Massimo D'Antona"* 130

Zucchetti, E. 2005. La disoccupazione. Letture, percorsi, politiche, Milano, Vita e Pensiero

Index

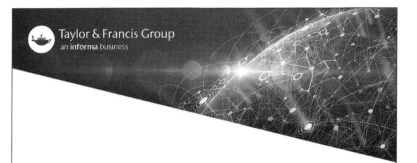